Mes petites lunes
Ariane Lauzon

WOODLAND WONDERS

Tuva Publishing
www.tuvapublishing.com

Address Merkez Mah. Cavusbasi Cad. No.71
Cekmekoy - Istanbul 34782 / Türkiye
Tel +9 0216 642 62 62

Woodland Wonders

First Print 2025 / March

All Global Copyrights Belong to
Tuva Tekstil ve Yayıncılık Ltd.

Content Sewing

Editor in Chief Ayhan DEMİRPEHLİVAN
Project Editor Kader DEMİRPEHLİVAN
Author Ariane LAUZON
Technical Editors Leyla ARAS
Graphic Designers Ömer ALP, Abdullah BAYRAKÇI, Tarık TOKGÖZ, Yunus GÜLDOĞAN
Photography Tuva Publishing, Ariane LAUZON

All rights are reserved. No part of this publication may be reproduced, stored in a retrieval system, or transmitted in any form or by any means, electronic, mechanical, photocopying, recording, or otherwise, without prior written consent of the publisher. The copyrights of the designs in this book are protected and may not be used for any commercial purpose.

ISBN 978-605-7834-90-4

 TuvaPublishing

Welcome to my world. A world where art, textile, and design intertwine. A world that has brought so much happiness into my life.

Creating has always been close to my heart, and as I taught myself to sew when I first became a mother, doll-making rapidly became my favorite medium. As I walked this path, I discovered the quiet poetry of making beauty comes to life. There is something truly special about imagining and pouring love and care into crafting a unique object that will be cherished for years.

I am so happy you've decided to join me on this journey and deeply touched that Mes Petites Lunes dolls will be handled and colored by so many other hands all over the world. This is so precious.

Kindly

Ariane

Bear	16	Fox	22	Hedgehog	28
Raccoon	34	Fawn	40	Mini Bear	46
Pinafore Dress/Overalls	52	Axel Dress/Jumpsuit	58	Turtleneck	62

Romane Jumpsuit 66	Bobbie Jacket 72	Tail-Fit Harem Pants 78
Suspender Pants 82	Beret 88	Accordion Bow 92
Pinwheel Bow 96	Mini Maddy Jumpsuit/Dress 100	Mini Skirt & Ruffle Collar 104

General Instructions

WASHING

For Outfits
Pre-wash the fabric if the outfits will be handled or washed frequently. Pre-washing prevents shrinkage after sewing and enhances the appearance of certain fabrics, such as linen and muslin.

For Dolls
Pre-washing the fabric is unnecessary for dolls. Dolls are not designed for machine washing or drying, as the delicate face embroidery can be damaged. If cleaning is needed, hand washing is recommended. Hand washing is gentle and should not affect the doll's shape or structure.

IRONING

Iron the fabric before cutting and sewing to remove any creases and ensure precise cutting. Smooth, wrinkle-free fabric makes it easier to align pattern pieces accurately. Adjust the iron's heat setting to match the fabric type, and use a pressing cloth for delicate fabrics to prevent damage.

SEAM ALLOWANCE

The seam allowance is the distance between the stitching line and the raw edge of the fabric. Seam allowances are already included in these patterns, so there is no need to add them. All pattern pieces include a ⅜ in (0.9 cm) seam allowance unless otherwise specified.

GRAINLINE

The grainline runs lengthwise, parallel to the selvedge edges of the fabric. It is typically in the opposite direction of the fabric's stretch. The cutting layout for the pattern is determined based on the grainline.

OPPOSITES PIECES

Opposite pieces are two fabric pieces that mirror each other. To create them, either fold the fabric in half and cut the pattern piece through both layers at once, or, if cutting on a single layer of fabric, flip the pattern piece to create the mirrored (opposite) piece.

RIGHT SIDES TOGETHER

"Right sides together" or "Right sides facing" means placing the fabric pieces with their right (outer) sides facing each other. The right side is the side of the fabric meant to be visible on the finished garment. Sewing with the right sides together ensures that the seam allowance and stitching will be on the wrong (inner) side of the garment when turned right-side out.

STITCH LENGTH

Using a stitch length of 2.5 mm is recommended for this pattern, unless specified otherwise. This setting is typically the default on most sewing machines.

BACKSTITCHING

Backstitch at the beginning and end of each seam to secure it and prevent it from unraveling. Use the reverse function on the sewing machine to sew a few stitches backward over the same area after sewing forward.

Embroidery Techniques

SATIN STITCH

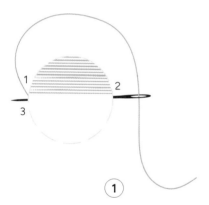

1
Bring the needle up at the edge of the shape.

2
Insert the needle into the fabric directly across on the opposite edge of the shape.

3
Bring the needle up through the fabric on the first edge of the shape, just below the first stitch.

4
Continue alternating between steps 2 and 3, stitching from one edge to the other, until the shape is filled with stitches.

KNOTLESS START

1
Fold the thread in half.

Pull the tails through the eye of the needle.

2
Insert the needle through the fabric at the starting point.

Pull the thread until there is a small loop left on the opposite side.

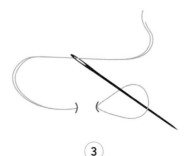

3
Pass the needle through the loop.

4
Pull the thread tight.

EMBROIDERY TECHNIQUES   9

SLIP KNOT

①

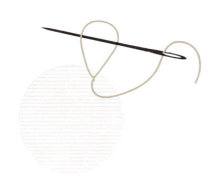

②

Weave the needle under a stitch near the end, pulling the thread until a small loop forms.

Pass the needle through the loop and pull tight to secure the thread.

BACKSTITCH

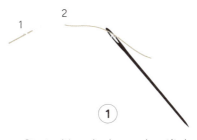

① Start with a single regular stitch.

② Bring the needle up a stitch length away from the end of the first stitch.

③ Insert the needle back down into the hole at the end of the previous stitch.

Bring the needle back up a stitch length away from the hole where the thread comes out. Repeat step 3 and 4.

RUNNING STITCH

① Bring the needle up through the fabric at your starting point.

② Insert the needle down into the fabric a stitch length away.

③ Bring the needle up a stitch length ahead, and continue stitching along the line.

LADDER STITCH OR INVISIBLE STITCH

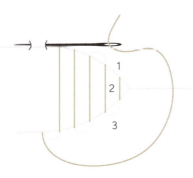

① Secure the thread at the edge of the seam allowance at one end of the opening.

② Position the needle on the opposite side of the opening, directly across from the hole where the thread exits.

③ Insert the needle into the fabric fold and bring it out ⅛ in (3 mm) further along the edge of the seam fold. Continue alternating between steps 2 and 3, stitching across and along the seam folds, until reaching the end of the opening.

10 EMBROIDERY INSTRUCTIONS   nose and mouth

Nose & Mouth Embroidery

1
To embroider the nose of all animals, cut a 22 in (55 cm) piece of embroidery thread. (If you're using 6-strand embroidery floss, I suggest splitting the thread in half and stitching with three strands to create thinner lines.) Fold the thread in half and pull both ends through the eye of the needle.

Bring the needle down into the fabric at the far right of the doll's nose and bring it up directly across on the opposite edge. Pull the thread until there is a small loop left on the right side and pass the needle through the loop (knotless start) and pull again.

2
Then, bring the needle into the fabric passing through the same hole where the loop came out and bring the needle out on the opposite side just below the first stitch. Pull tight to hide the knot inside the doll.

3
Continue stitching the nose until the shape is filled using the satin stitch. (Refer to Embroidery techniques p.8).

4
On the last satin stitch, bring the needle up at the bottom of the vertical line.

5
Then, bring the needle down at the base of the nose along the central seam and bring it up at the left corner of the mouth.

6
Bring the needle down at the bottom of the vertical line and bring it up at the right side of the mouth.

EMBROIDERY INSTRUCTIONS   11

7
Finally, bring the needle down again at the bottom of the vertical line and up at the top corner of the nose.

8
Finish with a slip knot. To do so, begin by bringing the needle under the closest stitch to the thread.

9
Then, pass the needle through the formed loop.

10
Pull to tighten the knot.

11
To hide the knot, bring the needle into the fabric passing through the hole of the stitch you use for the slip knot and bring the needle out a couple of inches away. Pull tight to tuck the knot inside.

12
Cut the remaining thread.

EMBROIDERY INSTRUCTIONS

Eye Embroidery

1
To embroider the eyes, cut a 22 in (55 cm) piece of black embroidery thread. (If you're using 6-strand embroidery floss, I suggest splitting the thread in half and stitching with three strands to create thinner lines.) Fold the thread in half and pull the tails through the eye of the needle.

Start by bringing the needle down into the fabric at the top far right of the eye and bring it up directly across on the opposite edge. Pull the thread until there is a small loop left on the right side and pass the needle through the loop (knotless start) and pull again.

2
Bring the needle into the fabric passing through the same hole where the loop came out and bring the needle up on the opposite side just below the first stitch. Pull tight to hide the knot into the doll.

3
Continue stitching until the shape is filled using the satin stitch. (Refer to Embroidery techniques p.8.)

4
On the last satin stitch, bring the needle up at the top center of the eye.

5
Outline the eye using the backstitch. (Refer to Embroidery techniques p.9.)

6
(This step is optional) On the last backstitch, bring the needle down into the fabric and up at the eyelashes and stitch them.

EMBROIDERY INSTRUCTIONS   13

7
Then, bring the needle back up close to the outline of the eye and finish with a slip knot. (Refer to Embroidery techniques p.9.) To hide the knot, bring the needle into the fabric passing through the hole of the stitch you use for the slip knot and bring the needle out a couple of inches away. Pull tight to tuck the knot inside. Repeat for the other eye.

8
Cut the remaining threads.

9
The easiest way to blush the cheeks is to color them using a pink color pencil. This method will fade over time but it always gives a soft and pretty result.

Another option is to use fabric paint. This method has the advantage of lasting over time but it could also be a disaster if you don't apply it correctly.

If you decide to use paint, wet your brush first, wipe it off, then take a very small amount of paint and make gentle circles on your doll's cheeks. Try it on a piece of fabric first before applying it to your doll.

14 HANDSEWING INSTRUCTIONS   Ladder Stitch

Closing the opening

1
To close the opening, begin by threading the needle with both ends of a folded thread.

Attach the thread to the folded edge of the opening using the knotless start method. (Refer to Embroidery techniques p.8.)

2
Hand-sew the opening closed using the ladder stitch. (Refer to Embroidery techniques p.8.)

3
When reaching the end of the opening, pull tight and finish with a slip knot. (Refer to Embroidery techniques p.8.) To make the knot, bring the needle under the closest stitch to the thread and pass it through the formed loop, as shown in the picture.

Pull to tighten the knot.

4
To hide the knot inside the doll, bring the needle into the fabric passing through the hole of the stitch you used for the slip knot and bring the needle out a couple of inches away. Pull tight to tuck the knot inside and cut the remaining thread.

Bear

Meet Charlotte and Charles, the not-even-grumpy bear cubs - camping enthusiasts with a fondness for roasted marshmallows. As the fire crackles, they savor golden-brown s'mores, but when night falls, they stash their treats away from hungry bears, resisting the sweet allure of chocolate.

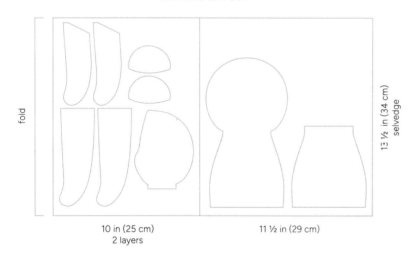

CUTTING LAYOUT

- FABRIC
A piece 31 ½ in (79 cm) wide
x 13 ½ in (34 cm) long for the body

  Recommended fabric
  For the body, I suggest a medium-weight woven fabric, such as cotton, linen or a blend of both.

- STUFFING
Approximately 5 oz (150 g) of stuffing. This can be polyester stuffing, available in most craft stores or large retailers. Natural fibers such as carded wool can also be used.

- SEWING THREAD
100% polyester thread that matches the color of the fabric

- EMBROIDERY THREAD
for eyes, nose and small hairs

- EMBROIDERY NEEDLE

- FABRIC PAINT
or color pencil / blush for the cheeks

- TURNING TOOL
(it could simply be a chopstick)

- ERASABLE FABRIC PEN

- SEWING MACHINE

- FABRIC SCISSORS

- PINKING SHEARS (optional)

- PINS

- RULER

- IRON

18 BEAR

SEAM ALLOWANCE
⅜ in (0.9 cm) seam allowance included unless otherwise specified

1
Cut out the pattern pieces from the fabric following the grainline and take note of the markings (the small lines printed on the pattern pieces). You must have 1 back piece, 1 front piece, 2 face pieces, 4 leg pieces, 4 arm pieces, and 4 ear pieces.

2
With right sides facing, pin each pair of legs and arms and sew along the line as shown.

3
Trim the seam allowance of the curves of the legs and arms to reduce bulk.

4
Turn the legs and the arms right side out using a loop turner or a chopstick.

5
Align the seams at the center for the legs and at the sides for the arms, and iron flat.

6
Begin to stuff both legs and arms by pushing small amounts of stuffing toward the feet and hands. Make sure the feet and hands are stuffed firmly and then continue stuffing up to 1 in (2.5 cm) before opening.

7
Align once again the seams at the center for the legs, pin and sew along the raw edges to close the opening.

8
With right sides facing, pin the two face pieces together and sew along the edge as shown.

9
Press the seam open as it is in the picture. With right sides facing, sew the face and the front piece together, as shown.

10
With right sides facing, pin each pair of ears in place and sew along the edge of fabric, as shown, with a 3/16 in (0.5 cm) seam allowance.

11
Turn both ears right side out. Fold the center of each ear by ³⁄₁₆ in (0.5 cm).

12
Sew to secure the fold near the edge.

13
Pin the ears on the right side of the face at the ear markings indicated on the pattern. Align the raw edges and secure the ears in place by sewing close to the edge.

14
Pin the arms between the arm markings and the neck seam. The top edge of the arms should extend about ⅜ in (0.9 cm) beyond the neck seam so that the arms are aligned with the neck when the doll is turned over. Sew to secure near the edge.

15
With right sides facing, place the front of the doll on top of the back and pin in place. Ensure the neck markings are aligned with the neck seam and the center head marking is aligned with the central seam of the face.

16
Sew carefully all the way around leaving a 1½ in (4 cm) gap on the side at the opening markings for stuffing.

17
Trim the seam allowance around the head and neck using pinking shears or by making small triangle cuts. Trim also the tip of nose to reduce bulk.

18
Turn the doll right side out and ensure that everything is properly sewn.

19
Stuff firmly the head by the bottom of the body. Ensure that the head is round with no crease. You can push small amounts of stuffing toward the sides and the nose to shape the face.

20
Fold the bottom edge 1 in (2.5 cm) toward the inside of the body and iron.

21
With the front of the doll facing toward you, insert ¾ in (2 cm) of each leg into the body and pin in place. Ensure the feet are facing upward and the legs are the same length. Sew the legs by stitching a straight line near the bottom of the body.

22
Stuff the rest of the body.

23
Hand-sew the opening closed using the ladder stitch. (Refer to p.14.)

24
To draw the face, use an erasable fabric pen. Measure 3 ⅜ in (8.5 cm) down from the top head seam along the central face seam, and place a pin to mark the spot.

25
Trace a rectangle as for the nose measuring ⅝ in (1.5 cm) wide by 3/16 in (0.5 cm) long, centered on the seam directly below the pin.

For a smiling mouth, draw a line 3/16 in (0.5 cm) downward along the central seam, then draw a diagonal line ⅜ in (0.9 cm) tilted up on each side. For a neutral mouth, draw a diagonal line ⅜ in (0.9 cm) tilted down on each side, directly below the base of the nose.

26
Move the pin ⅜ in (0.9 cm) upward along the central seam, then place the ruler horizontally below the pin. Measure 1 ⅜ in (3.5 cm) to each side, and mark each spot with a dot.

27
Draw a circle of ¼ in (0.6 cm) diameter around each dot. (To draw round circles and eyelashes, you can use the template provided in the pattern.)

28
Embroider the face following the steps on pages 10-13.

29.
Color the cheek using the method described on page 13.

Fox

Meet Bernadette and Bernard, the mountaineering fox pair - experts at climbing snowy peaks with skill and flair. Snowboarders and hikers, they spread joy with delight, traveling far and wide for fresh air and light.

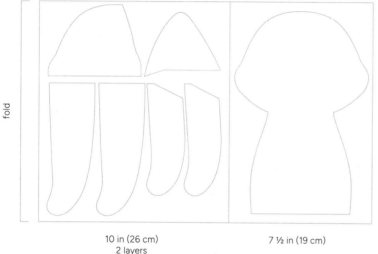

CUTTING LAYOUT
MAIN FABRIC (SHADES OF ORANGE)

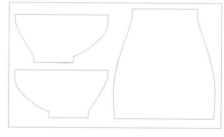

INNER EAR FABRIC

CONTRAST FABRIC (CREAM-BEIGE)

- **FABRIC**
  A piece 27 ½ in (71 cm) wide x 11 ½ in (29 cm) long as the main fabric (shades of orange)

  A piece 11 in (28 cm) wide x 6 ½ in (17 cm) long as the contrast fabric (beige - cream)

  A piece 9 in (24 cm) wide x 4 in (10 cm) long for the inner ears (minky)

  Recommended fabric
  For the body, I suggest a medium-weight woven fabric, such as cotton, linen or a blend of both.

- **STUFFING**
  Approximately 5 oz (150 g) of stuffing. This can be polyester stuffing, available in most craft stores or large retailers. Natural fibers such as carded wool can also be used.

- **SEWING THREAD**
  100% polyester thread that matches the color of the fabrics

- **EMBROIDERY THREAD**
  for eyes, nose and small hairs

- **EMBROIDERY NEEDLE**

- **FABRIC PAINT**
  or color pencil / blush for the cheeks

- **TURNING TOOL**
  (it could simply be a chopstick)

- **ERASABLE FABRIC PEN**

- **SEWING MACHINE**

- **FABRIC SCISSORS**

- **PINKING SHEARS** (optional)

- **PINS**

- **RULER**

- **IRON**

24　FOX

SEAM ALLOWANCE
⅜ in (0.9 cm) seam allowance included
unless otherwise specified

1
Cut out the pattern pieces from the fabric following the grainline and take note of the markings (the small lines printed on the pattern pieces). You must have 1 back piece, 1 front piece, 2 upper face pieces, 2 lower face pieces, 4 leg pieces, 4 arm pieces and 4 ear pieces.

2
With right sides facing, pin each pair of legs and arms and sew along the line as shown.

3
Trim the seam allowance around the curves of the legs and arms to reduce bulk.

4
Turn the legs and the arms right side out using a chopstick. Align the seams at the center for the legs and at the sides for the arms, and iron flat.

5
Begin to stuff both legs and arms by pushing small amounts of stuffing toward the feet and hands. Ensure the feet and hands are stuffed firmly and then continue stuffing up to 1 in (2.5 cm) before opening.

6
Align once again the seams at the center for the legs, pin and sew along the raw edges to close the opening.

7
With right sides facing, pin the two upper face pieces together and sew along the edge as shown.

8
Repeat Step 7 with the two lower face pieces.

9
With right sides facing, pin the two assembled pieces of the face (upper and lower) together, aligning the straight edges and central seams.

10
Sew along the edge of fabric, as shown.

11
With right sides facing, sew the face and the front piece together, as shown.

12
With right sides facing, pin each pair of ears together and sew along the edge of fabric, as shown.

13
Turn both ears right side out. Fold the longest side of each ear ⅜ in (1 cm) toward the inside as shown, then sew to secure near the edge.

14
Pin the ears on the right side of the face at the ear markings (all markings are indicated on the pattern). The inner sides of the ears must face the right side of the face, with the folded edges pointing inward. Secure the ears by stitching near the edge.

15
Pin the arms between the arm markings and the neck seam. The top edge of the arms should extend about ⅜ in (0.9 cm) beyond the neck seam so that the arms are aligned with the neck when the doll is turned over. Sew to secure.

16
With right sides facing, place the front of the doll on top of the back and pin in place.

17
Ensure the neck markings are aligned with the neck seam and the center head marking is aligned with the central seam of the face.

18
Sew carefully all the way around leaving a 1 ½ in (4 cm) gap on the side for stuffing.

19
Trim the seam allowance around the head and neck using pinking shears or by making small triangle cuts. Trim also the tip of the nose to reduce bulk.

20
Turn the doll right side out.

21
Stuff firmly the head by the bottom of the body. You can push small amounts of stuffing toward the sides of the head and toward the nose to shape the face.

22
Fold the bottom edge 1 in (2.5 cm) toward the inside of the body and iron.

23
With the front of the doll facing toward you, insert ¾ in (2 cm) of each leg into the body and pin in place. Ensure the feet are facing upward and the legs are the same length.

24
Sew the legs by stitching a straight line near the bottom of the body. Stuff the rest of the body.

25
Hand-sew the opening closed using the ladder stitch. (Refer to p.14)

26
To draw the face, use an erasable fabric pen. For the nose, trace a rectangle measuring ⅝ in (1.5 cm) long by 3⁄16 in (0.5 cm) wide centered on the face seam.

For a smiling mouth, draw a line 3⁄16 in (0.5 cm) downward along the central seam, then draw a diagonal line ⅜ in (0.9 cm) tilted up on each side. For a neutral mouth, draw a diagonal line ⅜ in (0.9 cm) tilted down on each side, directly below the base of the nose.

27
For the eyes, measure 1 ½ in (4 cm) on each side from the central seam, ⅜ in (1 cm) above the horizontal seam, and mark each spot with a dot. Draw a circle of ¼ in (0.6 cm) diameter around each dot. Dots should be at the center. (To draw round circles and eyelashes, you can use the template provided in the pattern.)

28
Embroider the face and color the cheeks following the steps on page 10-13.

Hedgehog

Meet Rocky and Roxy, the spiky rock stars - strumming their guitars, reaching for the stars. Inspired by the timeless hum of The Beatles' strings and the raw energy the Rolling Stones bring, they weave the old into something new, creating music that feels both fresh and true.

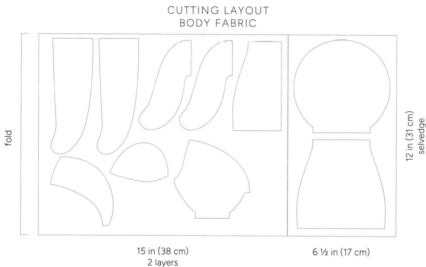

- **FABRIC**
  A piece 36 ½ in (93 cm) wide x 12 in (31 cm) long for the body

  A piece 12 ½ in (32 cm) wide x 7 in (18 cm) long for the textured fabric (minky or sherpa)

  A piece 8 in (20 cm) wide x 3 in (8 cm) long for the inner ear

  Recommended fabric
  For the body, I suggest a medium-weight woven fabric, such as cotton, linen or a blend of both.

- **STUFFING**
  Approximately 5 oz (150 g) of stuffing. This can be polyester stuffing, available in most craft stores or large retailers. Natural fibers such as carded wool can also be used.

- **SEWING THREAD**
  100% polyester thread that matches the color of the fabrics

- **EMBROIDERY THREAD** (floss)
  for eyes, nose and small hairs

- **EMBROIDERY NEEDLE**

- **FABRIC PAINT**
  or color pencil / blush for the cheeks

- **TURNING TOOL**
  (it could simply be a chopstick)

- **ERASABLE FABRIC PEN**

- **SEWING MACHINE**

- **FABRIC SCISSORS**

- **PINKING SHEARS** (optional)

- **PINS**

- **RULER**

- **IRON**

HEDGEHOG

SEAM ALLOWANCE
3/8 in (0.9 cm) seam allowance included unless otherwise specified

1
Cut out the pattern pieces from the fabric following the grainline and take note of the markings (the small lines printed on the pattern pieces). You must have 2 face pieces, 4 forehead pieces, 2 head pieces, 2 back pieces, 1 front piece, 4 leg pieces, 4 arm pieces and 4 ear pieces.

2
With right sides facing, pin each pair of legs and arms and sew along the line as shown.

3
Trim the seam allowance around the curves of the legs and arms.

4
Turn the legs and the arms right side out using a loop turner or a chopstick.

5
Align the leg seams at the center and arm seams at the sides, and iron flat.

6
Stuff both legs and arms. Start by firmly stuffing the feet and hands, then continue stuffing up to 1 in (2.5 cm) from the opening.

7
Align once again the leg seams at the center, and sew along the raw edges to close the opening.

8
Lay the two head pieces with the right side of fabric facing up.

9
Place the textured fabric on top of the main fabric, with the right side of the main fabric facing the wrong side of the textured fabric. Sew a few stitches along the top, bottom, and sides, near the edges, to secure the pieces together.

10
With right sides facing, pin the two back pieces together and sew along the line, leaving a 1 ½ in (4 cm) gap at the opening markings for stuffing.

11
With right sides facing, sew the back piece and the head piece together.

12
Place each textured fabric forehead piece on top of the corresponding main fabric piece, with the right side of the main fabric facing the wrong side of the textured fabric, as done previously for the head. Sew a few stitches near the edges to secure the layers, as shown.

13
With right sides facing, place each forehead piece on top of the corresponding face piece. Align the bottom edge (concave curve) of the forehead piece with the top edge of the face piece, as shown, and pin.

14
Sew along the edge of fabric, as shown.

15
It should now look like this.

16
With right sides facing, pin the two face pieces together, ensuring both forehead seams are aligned, and sew along the edge of fabric, as shown.

17
With right sides facing, sew the face and the front piece together, as shown.

18
With right sides facing, pin each pair of ears and sew along the line, as shown, with a ³⁄₁₆ in (0.5 cm) seam allowance.

19
Turn both ears right side out. Fold the longest side of each ear 1 ¼ in (3 cm) toward the inside (the folded sides of the ears must face each other). Sew to secure the folds, near the edge.

20
Position the ears on the right side of the face, aligning them with the ear markings and extending them ¾ in (2 cm) above the forehead. The inner ears must face the right side of the face, with the folded edges upward. Sew to secure near the edge.

21
Pin the arms between the arm markings and the neckline. The top edge of the arms should be perfectly aligned with the neckline. (All markings are indicated on the pattern.) Sew to secure at ³⁄₁₆ in (0.5 cm) from the edge.

22
With right sides facing, place the front of the doll on top of the back and pin in place.

23
Ensure both necklines are aligned and the head center marking is aligned with the central seam of the face.

24
Sew carefully all the way around, as shown.

25
Trim the seam allowance around the head and neck using pinking shears or by making small triangle cuts.

26
Turn the doll right side out. Ensure that everything is properly sewn, then use your hands or a chopstick to press along the inside of the seams to shape the face and nose.

27
Stuff firmly the head by the bottom of the body. Make sure that the head is round with no crease. Use a chopstick to push more stuffing toward the nose to make it pointier.

28
Fold the bottom edge 1 in (2.5 cm) toward the inside of the body and iron.

29
With the front of the doll facing toward you, insert ¾ in (2 cm) of each leg into the body and pin in place. Ensure the feet are facing upward and the legs are the same length.

30
Sew the legs by stitching a straight line near the bottom of the body.

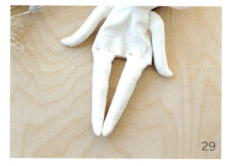

HEDGEHOG 33

31
Stuff the rest of the body starting by the neck area ensuring there are no creases at the sides and at the back of the neck. Stuff firmly the corner of the body close to the legs and the center of the body.

32
Hand-sew the opening closed using the ladder stitch. (Refer to p.14)

33
To draw the face, use an erasable fabric pen.

For the nose, trace an oval about ½ in (1.25 cm) in lenght and ¼ in (0.6 cm) in width at the tip of the raised (pointed) part of the face. From the base of the nose, trace a line 3⁄16 in (0.5 cm) downward along the central seam, then trace a diagonal line 3⁄8 in (0.9 cm) tilted up on each side.

34
Place a pin 3⁄8 in (1 cm) above the top of the nose along the central seam.

35
Place a measuring tape horizontally directly below the pin. Measure 1 ½ in (4 cm) to each side from the pin, following the grain of the fabric, and mark each spot with a dot.

36
Draw a circle of ¼ in (0.6 cm) diameter around each dot. Dots should be at the center. (To draw round circles and eyelashes, you can use the template provided in the pattern.)

37
Embroider the face and color the cheeks following the steps on pages 10-13.

Raccoon

Meet Tommie and Tom, the raccoons - masters of reuse, turning scraps into treasures with nothing to lose. Experts in composting and sorting with care, they give old things new life, keeping waste rare.

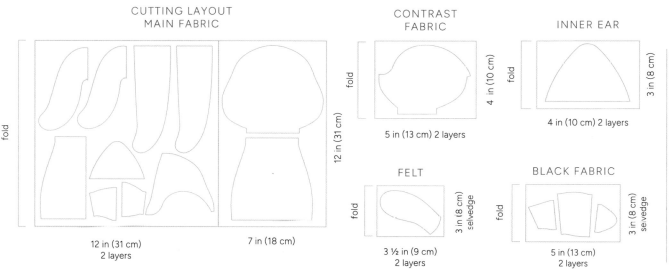

- **FABRIC**
  A piece 31 in (80 cm) wide x 12 in (31 cm) long as the main fabric

  A piece 10 in (26 cm) wide x 4 in (10 cm) long as the contrast fabric

  A piece 10 in (26 cm) wide x 3 in (8 cm) long for the black fabric

  A piece 8 in (20 cm) wide x 3 in (8 cm) long for the inner ear (minky)

  A piece 7 in (18 cm) wide x 3 in (8 cm) long of black felt fabric

  Recommended fabric
  For the body, I suggest a medium-weight woven fabric, such as cotton, linen or a blend of both.

- **STUFFING**
  Approximately 5 oz (150 g) of stuffing. This can be polyester stuffing, available in most craft stores or large retailers. Natural fibers such as carded wool can also be used.

- **SEWING THREAD**
  100% polyester thread that matches the color of the fabrics

- **EMBROIDERY THREAD**
  for eyes, nose and small hairs

- **EMBROIDERY NEEDLE**

- **FABRIC PAINT**
  or color pencil / blush for the cheeks

- **TURNING TOOL**
  (it could simply be a chopstick)

- **ERASABLE FABRIC PEN**

- **SEWING MACHINE**

- **FABRIC SCISSORS**

- **PINKING SHEARS** (optional)

- **PINS**

- **RULER**

- **IRON**

36 RACCOON

SEAM ALLOWANCE
⅜ in (0.9 cm) seam allowance included unless otherwise specified

1
Cut out the pattern pieces from the fabric following the grainline and take note of the markings (the small lines printed on the pattern pieces). You must have 2 upper face and 2 lower face pieces, 1 head piece, 2 back pieces, 1 front piece, 4 leg pieces, 4 arm pieces, 4 ear pieces, 10 tail pieces, and 2 eye patches.

2
With right sides facing, pin each pair of legs and arms and sew along the line as shown.

3
Trim the seam allowance around the curves of the legs and arms.

4
Turn the legs and the arms right side out using a chopstick and iron flat.

5
Stuff both legs and arms. Start by firmly stuffing the feet and hands, then continue stuffing up to 1 in (2.5 cm) from the opening.

6
Align the leg seams at the center and arm seams at the sides, and iron flat.

7
With right sides facing, pin each pair of ears in place and sew along the edge of fabric, as shown.

8
Turn both ears right side out. Fold one side of each ear ¾ in (2 cm) inward, and sew to secure near the edge.

9
With right side facing, place the first tail piece on top of the second, aligning the matching edges. (Refer to the numbers and markings on each pattern piece as a guide) Sew along the edge, as shown, with a 3⁄16 in (0.5 cm) seam allowance.

10
With right side facing, place the third tail piece on top of the second, aligning the matching edges. Sew as shown, with a 3⁄16 in (0.5 cm) seam allowance.

11
Repeat with the fourth and third piece.

12
Repeat with the fifth and fourth piece.

13
With right sides facing, pin the two tail pieces together, aligning all seams. Sew as shown, with a ³⁄₁₆ in (0.5 cm) seam allowance. Turn the tail right side out.

14
Place the tail downward on the right side of one back piece, aligning it with the tail markings. Lay the second back piece on top, right sides facing. Sew along the line, leaving a 1 ½ in (4 cm) gap at the opening markings for stuffing

15
With right sides facing, sew the head piece and the back piece together.

16
To assemble the face, place each upper face piece on top of its corresponding lower face piece, right sides together. Align the bottom edge of the upper face pieces with the top edge of the lower face pieces, and pin in place.

17
Here is a close-up of the pinned pieces. The bottom edge of the upper piece has a concave curve, while the top edge of the lower piece has a convex curve, which can make this step challenging.

18
To ensure the fabric ends match precisely, begin by sewing a few stitches at the end of the seam.

19
Sew along the edge with a a ³⁄₁₆ in (0.5 cm) seam allowance.

20
Place each eye patch on the corresponding face piece, aligning it with the markings indicated on the pattern, and pin in place. Sew around the patches with black thread, close to the edges, and finish with a zigzag stitch.

38 RACCOON

21
With right sides facing, pin the two face pieces together, ensuring both forehead seams are aligned, and sew along the edge of fabric, as shown.

22
With right sides facing, sew the face and the front piece together, as shown.

23
Pin the ears on the right side of the face at the ear markings. The inner sides of the ears must face the right side of the face, with the folded edges pointing inward. Secure the ears in place by sewing close to the edge.

24
Pin the arms between the arm markings and the neckline. The top edge of the arms should be aligned with the neckline. Sew to secure near the edge.

25
With right sides facing, place the front of the doll on top of the back and pin.

26
Ensure both necklines are aligned and the head center marking is aligned with the central seam of the face.

27
Sew carefully all the way around leaving the bottom open for stuffing.

28
Trim the seam allowance around the head and neck using pinking shears or by making small triangle cuts. Trim also the tip of the nose to reduce bulk.

29
Turn the doll right side out. Ensure that everything is properly sewn, then use your hands or a chopstick to press along the inside of the seams to shape the face and nose.

30
Stuff firmly the head by the bottom of the body. You can push small amounts of stuffing toward the sides of the head and toward the nose to shape the face.

31
Fold the bottom edge 1 in (2.5 cm) toward the inside of the body and iron.

32
With the front of the doll facing toward you, insert ¾ in (2 cm) of each leg into the body and pin in place. Ensure the feet are facing upward and the legs are the same length.

33
Sew the legs by stitching a straight line near the bottom of the body.

34
Stuff the rest of the body, starting with the neck area, ensuring there are no creases at the sides or back of the neck.

35
Hand-sew the opening closed using the ladder stitch. (Refer to p.14)

36
To draw the face, use an erasable fabric pen. Measure 4 in (10 cm) down from the top head seam along the central face seam. Place a pin to mark the spot.

37
Trace an oval for the nose measuring ⅝ in (1.5 cm) wide and ¼ in (0.6 cm) long, centered on the seam directly below the pin. From the base of the nose, trace a line 3⁄16 in (0.5 cm) downward along the central seam, then trace a diagonal line ⅜ in (0.9 cm) tilted up on each side.

38
Move the pin ¾ in (2 cm) upward along the central seam. Place a measuring tape horizontally directly below the pin and measure 1 ⅝ in (4 cm) to each side from the pin. Mark these spots with white chalk.

39
Draw a circle of ¼ in (0.6 cm) diameter at each marked spot.

40
Embroider the face following the steps on pages 10-13.

Fawn

Meet Louis and Louise, the nostalgic deers. They find joy on forest trails, away from gray, avoiding asphalt roads. During hunting season, the stags abandon their verdant exterior to enjoy their rustic interior. Wrapped up and secure, they watch their childhood classics of their old black and white TV's screen.

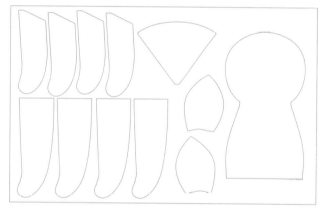
CUTTING LAYOUT
SHADES OF BROWN FABRIC

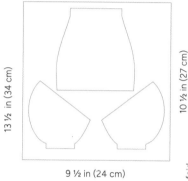
CREAM-BEIGE FABRIC

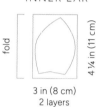
INNER EAR

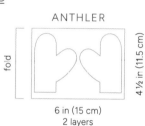
ANTHLER

— **FABRIC**
A piece of 22 ½ in (57 cm) wide x 13 ½ in (34 cm) long as your main fabric (shades of brown)

A piece of 9 ½ in (24 cm) wide x 10 ½ in (27 cm) long as your contrast fabric (beige - cream)

A piece of 6 in (16 cm) wide x 4 ¼ in (11 cm) long for the inner ears

A piece of 12 in (30 cm) wide x 4 ½ in (11.5 cm) long for the antlers

Recommended fabric
For the body, I suggest a medium-weight woven fabric, such as cotton, linen or a blend of both.

— **STUFFING**
Approximately 5 oz (150 g) of stuffing. This can be polyester stuffing, available in most craft stores or large retailers. Natural fibers such as carded wool can also be used.

— **SEWING THREAD**
100% polyester thread that matches the color of the fabrics

— **EMBROIDERY THREAD** (floss)
for eyes, nose and color spots

— **EMBROIDERY NEEDLE**

— **FABRIC PAINT**
or color pencil / blush for the cheeks

— **TURNING TOOL**
(it could simply be a chopstick)

— **ERASABLE FABRIC PEN**

— **SEWING MACHINE**

— **FABRIC SCISSORS**

— **PINKING SHEARS** (optional)

— **PINS**

— **RULER**

— **IRON**

42 FAWN

SEAM ALLOWANCE
⅜ in (0.9 cm) seam allowance included unless otherwise specified

1
Cut out the pattern pieces from the fabric following the grainline and take note of the markings (the small lines printed on the pattern pieces). You must have 1 back piece, 1 front piece, 2 face pieces, 1 forehead piece, 4 leg pieces, 4 arm pieces, 4 ear pieces and 4 antler pieces (optional).

2
With right sides facing, pin each pair of legs and arms and sew along the line as shown.

3
Trim the seam allowance around the curves of the legs and arms to reduce bulk.

4
Turn the legs and the arms right side out using a chopstick. Align the leg seams at the center and arm seams at the sides, and iron flat.

5
Stuff both legs and arms. Start by firmly stuffing the feet and hands, then continue stuffing up to 1 in (2.5 cm) from the opening.

6
Sew along the raw edges of the legs to close the opening.

7
With right sides facing, align the diagonal edge of one of the face pieces with one edge of the forehead. Sew along the line as shown, stopping at ⅜ in (0.9 cm) before reaching the end.

8
Repeat this step with the second face piece and the opposite edge of the forehead, always right sides together.

9
It should look like this.

10
Fold the face in half with right sides together. Push the forehead outward, folding it in half as well. Sew along the edge as shown, ensuring that both forehead seams are stitched over.

11
Verify that all parts are properly sewn, ensuring there are no unstitched areas around the nose (tip of the forehead).

12
With right sides facing, sew the face and the front piece together, as shown.

13
With right sides facing, pin each pair of ears and sew along the edge of fabric, with a ³⁄₁₆ in (0.5 cm) seam allowance.

14
Turn both ears right side out. Fold one side of each ear ⅜ in (1 cm) inward (the folded sides of the ears must face each other) and sew to secure near the edge.

15
Pin the ears on the right side of the face, aligning the edge of the folded sides with the forehead seams.

16
Align the raw edges and secure the ears in place by stitching near the edge.

17
Ensure that the folded sides of both ears are aligned with the forehead seams.

18
Pin the arms between the arm markings and the neck seam. The top edge of the arms should extend about ⅜ in (0.9 cm) beyond the neck seam so that the arms are aligned with the neck when the doll is turned over. Sew to secure near the edge.

19
To add antlers, place each pair of antler pieces right sides together. Sew along the edge with a ³⁄₁₆ in (0.5 cm) seam allowance. Trim the seam allowance with small cuts.

20
Turn the antlers right side out using a chopstick. Gently press the inside seam to shape. Stuff the antlers starting from the tip, then continue stuffing up to ½ in (1.2 cm) from the opening.

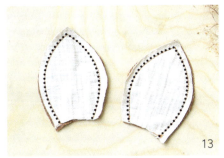

31
Position the antlers upside down on either side of the forehead center marking. Secure them in place by stitching near the edge.

32
With right sides facing, pin the front of the doll on top of the back.

33
Ensure the neck markings are aligned with the neck seam, and the center head and center forehead markings are aligned.

34
Sew carefully all the way around leaving a 1 ½ in (4 cm) gap on the side at the opening markings for stuffing.

35
Trim the seam allowance around the head and neck using pinking shears or by making small triangle cuts. Trim also the tip of the nose to reduce bulk.

36
Turn the doll right side out. Ensure that everything is properly sewn, then use your hands or a chopstick to press the inside seams to shape the face and nose.

37
Stuff firmly the head by the bottom of the body. Ensure that the head is round with no crease.

38
Fold the bottom edge 1 in (2.5 cm) toward the inside of the body and iron.

39
With the front of the doll facing toward you, insert ¾ in (2 cm) of each leg into the body and pin in place. Ensure the feet are facing upward and the legs are the same length. Sew the legs by stitching a straight line near the bottom of the body.

40
Stuff the rest of the body.

41
Hand-sew the opening closed using the ladder stitch. (Refer to p.14)

42
To draw the face, use an erasable fabric pen.

For the nose, trace a straight line from one side of the forehead to the other, at a distance of ⅜ in (0.9 cm) above its tip.

For a smiling mouth, draw a line 3/16 in (0.5 cm) downward along the central seam, then draw a diagonal line ⅜ in (0.9 cm) tilted up on each side. For a neutral mouth, draw a diagonal line ⅜ in (0.9 cm) tilted down on each side, directly below the base of the nose.

43
For the eyes, begin by measuring ⅜ in (1 cm) above the top of the nose and place a pin to mark the spot. Then, place the ruler horizontally below the pin and measure 1 ½ in (3.8 cm) to each side and mark each spot with a dot.

44
Draw a circle of ¼ in (0.6 cm) diameter around each dot. Dots should be at the center. (To help you draw round circles and eyelashes, you can use the template in the pattern section.) Embroider the face following the steps on pages 10-13.

45
Use the template in the pattern section to draw the color spots on the forehead of the doll. Thread the needle with both tails of a 60 in (150 cm) long beige folded thread. Secure the thread using the knotless start. (Refer p.8)

46
Fill the shapes using the satin stitch. (Refer p.8)

47
Stitch all color spots and finish with a slip knot. (Refer p.9)

48
Color the cheeks using the method described on page 13.

Mini Bear

Meet Charlotte and Charles, the mini bears - curious and bold, with adventurous stares. They're not just campers, they're explorers too, always seeking the world with a fresh point of view. While the fire crackles, they're off on their quest, collecting pinecones and finding the best.

CUTTING LAYOUT

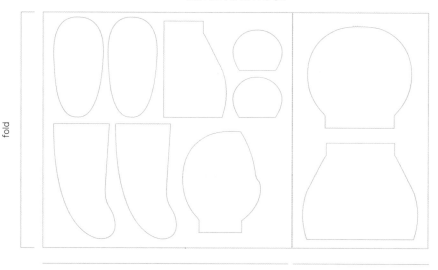

7 ½ in (19 cm)
2 layers

4 in (10 cm)

— FABRIC
A piece 19 in (48 cm) wide x 7 in (18 cm) long for the body

Recommended fabric
For the body, I suggest a medium-weight woven fabric, such as cotton, linen or a blend of both.

— STUFFING
Approximately 1 oz (30 g) of stuffing. This can be polyester stuffing, available in most craft stores or large retailers. Natural fibers such as carded wool can also be used.

— SEWING THREAD
100% polyester thread that matches the color of th fabrics

— EMBROIDERY THREAD
for eyes, nose and small hairs

— EMBROIDERY NEEDLE

— FABRIC PAINT
or color pencil / blush for the cheeks

— TURNING TOOL
(it could simply be a chopstick)

— ERASABLE FABRIC PEN

— SEWING MACHINE

— FABRIC SCISSORS

— PINKING SHEARS (optional)

— PINS

— RULER

— IRON

48 MINI BEAR

SEAM ALLOWANCE
⅜ in (0.9 cm) seam allowance included unless otherwise specified

1
Cut out the pattern pieces from the fabric following the grainline and take note of the markings (the small lines printed on the pattern pieces). You must have 1 front piece, 2 back pieces, 2 face pieces, 1 head piece, 4 leg pieces, 4 arm pieces, and 4 ear pieces.

2
With right sides facing, pin each pair of legs and arms together. Sew around the arms and legs, leaving a ½ in (1.3 cm) opening at the center for the arms and leaving the top of the legs open.

3
Trim the seam allowance of the curves of the legs and the arms to reduce bulk.

4
Turn both arms and legs right side out. To make this easier, insert a straw into the leg or arm and push it toward the closed end. Then, insert a chopstick into the straw from the opposite side and push the fabric outward.

5
Stuff the arms and legs, lightly filling the tops of the arms and stopping ⅜ in (1 cm) from the leg openings. Use tweezers for small parts.

6
Align the leg seams at the center and sew along the raw edges to close the opening. Set aside for later.

7
With right sides facing, pin the two face pieces together and sew along the edge, as shown.

8
With right sides facing, sew the face and the front piece together, as shown.

9
With right sides together, pin the two back pieces and sew along the edge as shown, leaving a 1 ¼ in (3 cm) gap at the opening markings for stuffing.

10
With right sides facing, sew the head and the back piece together, as shown.

MINI BEAR 49

11
With right sides facing, pin each pair of ears together and sew along the edge as shown, using a ³⁄₁₆ in (0.5 cm) seam allowance.

12
Turn both ears right side out. Fold the center of both ears by ³⁄₁₆ in (0.5 cm)

13
Sew to secure the fold near the edge.

14
Pin the ears on the right side of the face at the ear markings. Secure the ears in place by sewing close to the edge.

15
With right sides facing, pin the front of the doll on top of the back.

16
Ensure both necklines are aligned and the head center marking is aligned with the central seam of the face.

17
Sew carefully all the way around leaving the bottom open for turning.

18
Trim the seam allowance around the head and neck using pinking shears or by making small triangle cuts.

There are two options for sewing the legs (A and B)
OPTION A : Steps 19-21
OPTION B : Steps 22-23

19
OPTION A
This option hides the legs seam, which is ideal if not dressing the doll, but makes turning it out more difficult.

Place both legs in front of you, upside down with the feet facing upward toward the face.

20
OPTION A
Insert the legs inside the body, aligning their tops with the bottom edge, pin and sew the legs in place by stitching a straight line, as shown.

50 MINI BEAR

21
OPTION A
Turn the doll right side out, starting with the legs and gently pushing the head through.

22
OPTION B
This option shows the leg seam. Turn the body right side out. You can either stuff the head now or later. Fold the bottom edge ⅜ in (1 cm) toward the inside of the body and iron.

23
OPTION B
With the doll facing you, insert ⅜ in (1 cm) of each leg into the body, pin, ensuring the feet face up and legs are even. Sew the legs in place with a straight stitch near the bottom.

24
Stuff the doll through the opening.

25
Hand-sew the body and the arm openings closed using the ladder stitch. (Refer p.14)

26
Pin the arms at neck height on either side of the doll.

27
Thread a long needle with both ends of a folded thread. Insert the needle through the arm and body fabric, then bring it out further along the arm.

28
Pull the thread until a small loop remains on the right side and pass the needle through the loop (knotless start) and pull.

29
Pass the needle through the arm and body fabric again, bringing it out in front. Repeat a few times until the arm is firmly attached.

30
Bring the needle all the way through the doll's neck and out through the arm on the opposite side

31
Repeat the same steps to attach the second arm. Finish with a slip knot. (Refer p.9)

32
To draw the face, use an erasable fabric pen.

Draw a small rectangle for the nose at the tip of the raised part of the face centered with the face central seam. Then, measure ⅝ in (1.5 cm) to each side from the nose and ³⁄₁₆ in (0.5 cm) above it, and mark each spot with a dot.

33
To embroider the face, cut a 18 in (45 cm) piece of black embroidery thread. (If you're using 6-strand embroidery floss, I suggest splitting the thread in half and stitching with three strands to create thinner lines.)

Embroider the nose following the steps on page 10. When the nose is filled with stitches, bring the needle at the right eye.

34
Embroider the right eye with three satin stitches. (Refer to page 8). The third stitch can be longer if desired. On the last stitch, bring the needle out at the left eye and stitch it in the same manner.

35
Either finish here with a slipknot (refer p.9) or stitch a mouth following the steps on pages 10-11.

36
Color the cheeks following the steps on page 13.

Pinafore Dress/Overalls

This cute pinafore can be a dress or overalls - add a ruffle for a feminine touch, or keep it simple for a more neutral look. Whichever way you choose, your doll will be ready to turn heads and steal hearts!

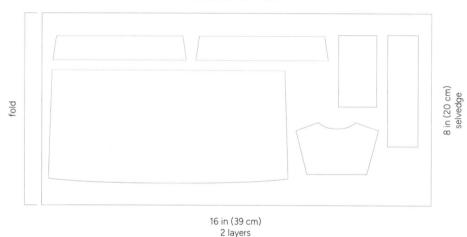

CUTTING LAYOUT
DRESS OPTION

16 in (39 cm)
2 layers

8 in (20 cm) selvedge

fold

- **FABRIC**
  A piece of fabric 32 in (78 cm) wide x 8 in (20 cm) long

  Recommended fabric
  This pattern works well with cotton, linen, hemp or any light to medium-weight fabric

- **SEWING THREAD**
  100% polyester thread that matches the color of the fabric

- **1/4 IN (0.6 CM) WIDE ELASTIC**
  2 x 3 ¼ in (8 cm) long pieces

- **SAFETY PIN**

- **SEWING MACHINE**

- **FABRIC SCISSORS**

- **PINS**

- **RULER**

- **IRON**

54　PINAFORE DRESS/OVERALLS

SEAM ALLOWANCE
⅜ in (0.9 cm) seam allowance included unless otherwise specified

1
Cut out the pattern pieces from the fabric following the grainline and take note of the markings (the small lines printed on the pattern pieces). You must have 2 front top pieces, 2 strap pieces, 2 front waistbands, 2 back waistbands, 2 ruffle pieces (optional) and 2 skirt or pants pieces.

2
Fold both straps in half lenghtwise and sew along the open edge with a ³⁄₁₆ in (0.5 cm) seam allowance.

3
Turn the straps right side out using a safety pin to guide one end through the tube.

4
Cut two 3 ¼ in (8 cm) elastic pieces and thread one through each casing.

5
Secure the elastic at both ends.

6
Pin the strap ends at the shoulder seams on one top piece. Sew each end ⅜ in (0.9 cm) from the side edges and ³⁄₁₆ in (0.5 cm) from the neckline.

7
To add ruffles to the front top, follow these steps. Skip to Step 12 if not adding ruffles. Fold each piece in half lengthwise. Stitch along one short end with a ³⁄₁₆ in (0.5 cm) seam allowance.

8
Turn the pieces right side out and iron.

9
To create the ruffles, set the machine to the widest stitch and sew a basting stitch along the raw edges. Do not backstitch at either end and leave a few inches of thread before clipping.

10
Carefully pull on one of the threads to gather the fabric. Pin both ruffles in place, aligning their raw edges with the side edges of the top and leaving a ⅜ in (1 cm) space at the top for the seam allowance.

PINAFORE DRESS/OVERALLS   55

11
Secure the ruffles in place, stitching at about ³⁄₁₆ in (0.5 cm) from the edges.

12
Pin the second front top piece on top, with right sides together.

13
Sew as shown, using a ³⁄₈ in (0.9 cm) seam allowance for the side edges and shoulder seams, and a ³⁄₁₆ in (0.5 cm) seam allowance for the neckline. Tuck the ruffles at the shoulder corners to prevent them from being caught.

14
Turn the top right side out and iron flat.

15
Place the two front waistband pieces with right sides together. Insert the top piece between them, aligning the center markings. (All markings are indicated on the pattern.) Pin in place.

16
Sew along the edge, as shown.

17
Place the two back waistband pieces (with the strap markings) with right sides together. Insert both straps between the waistband pieces, aligning them with the strap markings. Pin and sew along the edge.

18
To sew the front and back waistbands together, align the sides of the front waistband with the sides of the back waistband, with right sides facing, and sew along the side edges, as shown.

19
Press the seam allowances down on each side.

20
Turn the waistband right side out and iron flat. Sew a few stitches along each side seam to secure the two layers together.

56 PINAFORE DRESS/OVERALLS

21
Place the two skirt or pants pieces right sides together. Sew along the side edges as shown, and finish the seams using a serger or a zigzag stitch.

22
To create the ruffles, set the machine to the widest stitch and sew a basting stitch along the waistline near the edge. Do not backstitch at either end and leave a few inches of thread before clipping.

23
Carefully pull one of the threads to gather the fabric until the ruffle matches the waistband width. With the skirt or pants inside out and the top right side out and upside down, insert the waistband into the piece.

24
Align the raw edges and side seams, then gather the fabric evenly around the waistline. Pin all three layers of fabric together.

25
Sew around the waistline and finish the seam.

26
If making the pinafore overalls, skip to Step 27. To hem the bottom of the skirt, fold the bottom edge twice by ¼ in (0.6 cm) toward the inside, pin and sew close to the folded edge.

27
At this step, the pinafore overalls should look like this.

28
To hem the bottom of the pants, fold the bottom edge twice by ¼ in (0.6 cm) toward the inside, pin and sew close to the folded edge.

29
Turn the pants inside out. With the right sides of fabric facing, align the crotch and sew along the curve. Finish the seam.

30
Turn the grament right side out.

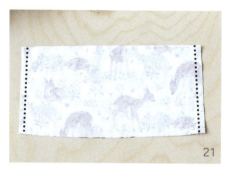

Axel Dress/Jumpsuit

The Axel jumpsuit or dress - wear it your way! With four straps to tie into sweet bows, it's a playful style for any doll who loves to move and groove!

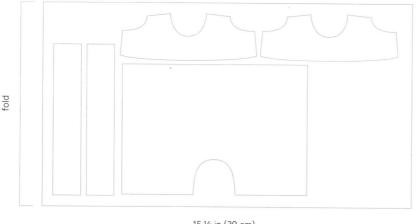

CUTTING LAYOUT
JUMPSUIT OPTION

fold

8 ½ in (22 cm) selvedge

15 ½ in (39 cm)
2 layers

— **FABRIC**
A piece 32 in (78 cm) wide
x 8 in (20 cm) long

Recommended fabric
This pattern works well with cotton, linen, hemp or any light to medium-weight fabric

— **SEWING THREAD**
100% polyester thread that matches the color of the fabric

— SEWING MACHINE

— SERGER (optional)

— FABRIC SCISSORS

— PINS

— IRON

60 AXEL DRESS/JUMPSUIT

SEAM ALLOWANCE
⅜ in (0.9 cm) seam allowance included unless otherwise specified

1
Cut out the pattern pieces from the fabric following the grainline. You must have 4 top pieces, 4 straps, and depending on the style you choose, 2 shorts or 2 skirt pieces.

2
Start by folding the straps in half lengthwise and ironing to mark the center. Then, fold one end of each strap ¼ in (0.6 cm) toward the wrong side and iron.

3
Next, fold both edges of each strap inward to meet in the middle, and iron to hold the folds in place.

4
Finally, fold each strap lengthwise again and pin to secure. Sew along the edge, stitching close to the open side. Tuck the folded ends inward to hide them within the seam.

5
Pin the unfinished ends of two straps on the right side of one top piece, ⅜ in (0.9 cm) from the armhole and 3⁄16 in (0.5 cm) from the neckline.

6
Secure the ends by stitching close to the edge, as shown. Repeat on a second top piece.

7
Place the remaining top pieces on top of the first ones, right sides together, aligning the edges, and pin in place.

8
Sew the pieces together, leaving the sides unsewn, and using a 3⁄16 (0.5 cm) seam allowance along the neckline.

9
Place the two tops with right sides together and sides open, then sew along the side edges.

10
Turn the assembled top right side out and press the seam allowances down on each side.

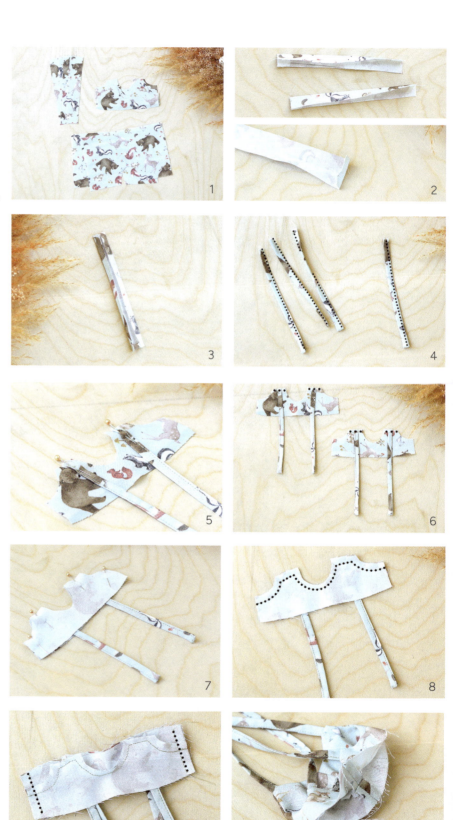

AXEL DRESS/JUMPSUIT

11
Iron the top flat. Sew a few stitches on each side seam to secure the two layers together.

12
Place the two skirt or shorts pieces with right sides together, pin and sew along the edges of fabric as shown.

13
Finish the seams using a serger or a zigzag stitch.

14
To create ruffles, set the machine to the widest stitch possible and sew a basting stitch along the waistline near the edge. Do not backstitch at either end and do not forget to leave a few inches of thread before clipping.

15
Carefully pull on one of the threads to gather the fabric until the width of the ruffle matches the width of the top piece. With the shorts or skirt turned inside out and the top right side out, insert the top into the piece.

16
Pin all three layers of fabric together, aligning raw edges and side seams.

17
Sew around the waistline and finish the seam with a serger or a zigzag stitch.

18
Turn the garment right side out. To hem the bottom, fold the bottom edge twice by ¼ in (0.6 cm) toward the inside and pin in place. Sew close to the folded edge along the bottom of each leg for the shorts or all the way around for the skirt. Dress is complete.

19
Turn the jumpsuit inside out. With right sides of fabric facing, align the crotch and sew along the curve. Finish the seam and flip it back right side out.

20
Tie the straps in bows and dress up your favorite Mes Petites Lunes dolls.

Turtleneck

This cozy turtleneck combines style and comfort in the sweetest way. Soft, snug, and perfect for layering, it'll keep your doll looking chic and feeling warm all season long!

CUTTING LAYOUT

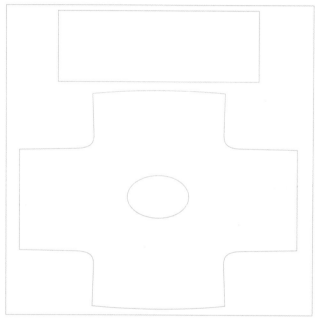

12 in (30 cm)
← stretch →

12 in (30 cm) selvedge

FABRIC
— A square piece 12 in (30 cm) side

Recommended fabric
This pattern works well with any knitted fabrics such as jersey, rib and fleece.

— SEWING NEEDLE
For stretch fabric

— SEWING THREAD
100% polyester thread that matches the color of the fabric

— SEWING MACHINE

— FABRIC SCISSORS

— PINS

64 TURTLENECK

SEAM ALLOWANCE
⅜ in (0.9 cm) seam allowance included unless otherwise specified

1
Cut out the pattern pieces from the fabric following the grainline. Be careful not to stretch the fabric when tracing and cutting. This might result in puckered seams. You must have 1 sweater piece and 1 neckband. (For knitted fabric, it's better to use a ballpoint stretch needle)

2
To hem the sleeves, fold the edge of both sleeves ¼ in (0.6 cm) toward the inside of fabric and sew along the edge. (A double fold is not necessary here since the fabric does not fray.)

3
With the right sides facing, fold the sweater in half, aligning all edges, pin and sew along both sides as shown.

4
Turn the sweater right side out. Fold the bottom edge ¼ in (0.6 cm) toward the inside and sew along the edge all the way around.

5
Fold the neckband in half widthwise with the right sides facing each other and sew along the edge.

6
Fold the neckband in half lengthwise so that the right side is facing out.

7
Turn the sweater inside out and insert the neckband upside down into the garment, aligning raw edges and aligning the neckband seam with the center back of the sweater. (The right sides of the sweater and the neckband are facing each other.) Pin all 3 layers of fabric together.

8
Sew around the neckline as shown.

9
Turn the turtleneck sweater right side out. Press the sleeve seam allowances down on each side and secure them in place by sewing a few back and forth stitches. Repeat for both sleeves.

Romane Jumpsuit

The Romane jumpsuit is as easy as it gets - elastic at the neck for a perfect fit, it's quick to slip on and off. A stylish choice that keeps your doll comfy and cute, without any fuss!

CUTTING LAYOUT

10 ½ in (27 cm)
2 layers

7 in (18 cm)

fold

12 in (31 cm) selvedge

- **FABRIC**
  A piece 28 in (72 cm) wide x 12 in (31 cm) long

  Recommended fabric
  This pattern works well with cotton, linen, hemp or any light to medium-weight fabric.

- **SEWING THREAD**
  100% polyester thread that matches the color of the fabric

- **1/4 IN (0.6 CM) WIDE ELASTIC**
  • 1 x 7 in (18 cm) piece long
  • 2 x 3 ½ in (9 cm) piece long
  • 2x 4 ¼ in (11 cm) piece long

- SAFETY PIN
- SEWING MACHINE
- SERGER (optional)
- FABRIC SCISSORS
- PINS
- IRON

68   ROMANE JUMPSUIT

SEAM ALLOWANCE
⅜ in (0.9 cm) seam allowance included unless otherwise specified

1
Cut out the pattern pieces from the fabric following the grainline and take note of the markings (the small lines printed on the pattern pieces). You have the option to choose between long or short pants and long or short sleeves. You must have 4 body pieces and 2 sleeve pieces.

2
Place each pair of body pieces together with right sides facing. Sew along the edges from the top down to the crotch point. This will create two assembled body pieces: one for the front and one for the back of the jumpsuit.

3
Finish the seams using a serger or a zigzag stitch.

4
With right sides facing, place the first sleeve onto one assembled body piece, aligning the armholes. Pin in place and sew along the armhole line as shown.

5
With right sides facing, align the armhole of the second assembled body piece with the second armhole of the first sleeve. Pin and sew along the armhole line as shown.

6
With right sides facing, align the armhole of the second sleeve with the second armhole of the second assembled body piece. Pin and sew along the armhole line as shown.

7
With right sides facing, align the two last unsewn armholes, pin and sew as shown.

8
Finish all 4 edges using a serger or using a zigzag stitch.

9
For gathered sleeves with an elastic casing, go to Step 13. For ruffled sleeves, hem the bottom edge without creating an elastic casing. To do so, fold the edge of each sleeve twice by ¼ in (0.6 cm) toward the inside and pin in place. Sew along the edge as close as possible to the folded edge.

ROMANE JUMPSUIT 69

10
Draw a line across the sleeve, parallel to the hem, ⅝ in (1.5 cm) from the edge of the sleeve hem. Cut out two 3 ¼ in (8 cm) long pieces of ¼ in (0.6 cm) wide elastic.

11
Sew the elastic directly along the traced line. Begin by securing the elastic at the start of the line, then stretch it so the end aligns with the end of the line. Continue to stretch the elastic as you sew.

12
Repeat steps 9-10-11 for the second sleeve.

13
To create gathered sleeves, fold the edge of each sleeve ¼ in (0.6 cm) toward the inside, fold again 5/16 in (0.8 cm), pin and sew close to the folded edge. Cut out two 3 ½ in (9 cm) long pieces of ¼ in (0.6 cm) wide elastic and thread them through the sleeve casings.

14
When the loose end of the elastic reaches the edge of the casing, secure it with a few back and forth stitches. Keep pushing the safety pin and secure it at the other end also.

15
Fold the jumpsuit in half, right sides together, pin and sew along both sides, as shown. Finish the seams with a serger or a zigzag stitch.

16
For gathered leg's hems with an elastic casing, skip to Step 20. For ruffled hems, simply fold the bottom edge of each leg twice by ¼ in (0.6 cm) toward the inside of fabric. Pin in place and sew along near the folded edges.

17
Draw a line across the leg opening, parallel to the hem, ⅝ in (1.5 cm) from it. Cut out two 4 ¼ in (11 cm) long pieces of ¼ in (0.6 cm) wide elastic. Mark the center of the elastic and align it with the leg seam, securing it in place with a pin.

70 ROMANE JUMPSUIT

18
Sew the elastic along the traced line. Begin by stretching the elastic to align with the start of the line, then sew while stretching it evenly to the midpoint, then to the end of line.

19
Repeat Steps 17-18-19 for the second leg.

20
For the elastic casing legs, fold the bottom edge of each leg ¼ in (0.6 cm) toward the inside of fabric, fold again 5/16 in (0.8 cm), pin and sew close to the folded edges. Cut out two 4 ¼ in (11 cm) long pieces of ¼ in (0.6 cm) wide elastic. Using a safety pin, thread one elastic through each casing and secure it at both ends to hold it in place.

21
With the jumpsuit turned inside out, align the crotch and sew along the curve. Finish the seam.

22
Turn the jumpsuit right side out. To make the elastic casing for the neck, fold the fabric around the neckline ¼ in (0.6 cm) toward the inside of fabric, then fold again 5/16 in (0.8 cm) and pin in place. Use as many pins as possible.

23
Sew around the neckline, stitching as close as possible to the folded edge leaving a 1 in (2.5 cm) opening at the back to insert the elastic. Cut out a 7 in (18 cm) long piece of ¼ in (0.6 cm) wide elastic. Using a safety pin, thread the elastic through the neckline casing.

24
When the loose end of the elastic reaches the opening of the casing, pin it to hold it in place. Keep pushing the safety pin through the casing all the way around until both ends meet.

25
Overlap both ends of the elastic about ⅜ in (1 cm) and sew them together.

26
Sew along the neckline as shown to close the opening.

27
You can hand-sew little buttons for a more dressed-up look. Voilà!

72 DOLL GARMENTS

Bobbie Jacket

The Bobbie jacket is the perfect mix of style and ease - featuring a velcro closure for quick on-and-off. Comfy, cozy, and ready to add a cool touch to any outfit!

CUTTING LAYOUT

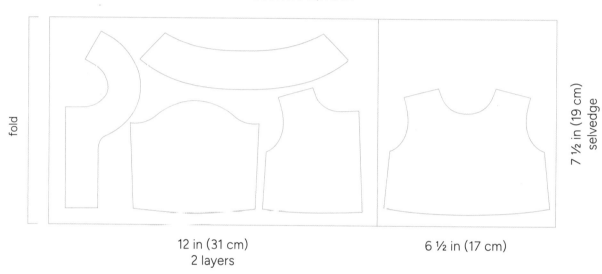

12 in (31 cm)
2 layers

6 ½ in (17 cm)

7 ½ in (19 cm) selvedge

fold

- **FABRIC**
  A piece 31 in (79 cm) wide x 7 ½ in (19 cm) long

  Recommended fabric
  This pattern works well with cotton, linen, or any light to medium-weight fabric.

- **SEWING THREAD**
  100% polyester thread that matches the color of the fabric

- **THIN VELCRO**
  2 x 1 in (2.5 cm) long

- **SEWING MACHINE**

- **SERGER** (optional)

- **FABRIC SCISSORS**

- **PINS**

- **IRON**

74   BOBBIE JACKET

SEAM ALLOWANCE
⅜ in (0.9 cm) seam allowance included
unless otherwise specified

1
Cut out the pattern pieces from the fabric following the grainline and take note of the markings (the small lines printed on the pattern pieces). You must have 1 back piece, 2 front pieces, 2 sleeve pieces, 2 collar pieces and 2 lining pieces.

2
With right sides facing, place the two front pieces on top of the back piece, aligning them at the shoulders. Pin and sew as shown. Finish the seams using a serger or a zigzag stitch.

3
Place the assembled piece flat on the work surface. Fold the back bodice in half to mark the center point, if not already marked.

4
With right sides facing, pin the two collar pieces together. Sew along the edges at ³⁄₁₆ in (0. 5 cm) from the edge leaving the neckline open, as shown. Trim the seam allowance by making small cuts along the curved edge and clip the corners diagonally.

5
Turn the collar right side out. Using a chopstick or similar tool, gently push out the corners and press the inside seams outward. Iron flat. Fold the collar in half to mark the center point.

6
Place the collar on the bodice, aligning the center markings of the collar and the back bodice. Pin the collar along the neckline. The collar should end approximately 2 cm from the edge of each front piece.

7
Sew along the neckline very close to the edge to secure the collar in place.

8
With right sides facing, pin the two lining pieces together and sew along the edge of fabric as shown. Finish the seam.

9
Finish the outer edge of the lining using a serger or a zigzag stitch.

10
With right sides facing, place the lining on top of the bodice, aligning its center seam with the center marking of the collar. Pin to secure. Align the necklines, corners, and front edges of both pieces and pin in place.

11
Sew along the edges and neckline as shown with a ⅜ in (0.5 cm) seam allowance.

12
Trim the seam allowance by making small cuts along the neckline and clip the corners diagonally. This helps the fabric stretch slightly, creating a smooth, rounded curve.

13
Turn the lining right side out. Using a chopstick, gently push out the corners and press the inside seams outward. Iron flat.

14
With right sides together, align the center marking of each sleeve with the shoulder seam of the bodice and pin it in place.

15
Then, pin each end of the sleeve's curved edge to the corresponding ends of the armhole. Gradually align the entire curved edge of the sleeve with the armhole, using multiple pins to secure the pieces evenly.

16
Sew along the curved edge, carefully aligning the fabric edges to ensure they remain matched. As you sew, use your fingers to gently guide the sleeve fabric along the curve, preventing any creases from forming. Repeat for the other sleeve.

17
To hem the sleeves, fold the edge of each sleeve twice by ¼ in (0.6 cm) toward the inside of fabric, and pin in place. Sew along the edge close to the folded edge.

18
With right sides together, fold the jacket in half along the shoulder seams, aligning the sleeves and sides. Pin in place. Sew along both sides from the sleeve hem to the bottom of the jacket. Finish the seams.

19
To hem the bottom of the jacket, fold the bottom edge twice by ¼ in (0.6 cm) toward the inside of fabric, and pin in place.

Note: If the fabric is too thick, finish the raw edge with a serger or zigzag stitch first. Then, fold the edge inward once by ¼ in (0.6 cm) and pin in place.

20
Sew along the line close to the folded edge.

21
Cut two pieces of thin Velcro, each 1 in (2.5 cm) long.

Note: When sewing Velcro, use a 2.0-length straight stitch to prevent stitch skipping.

22
Position the scratchy side (hook) of the Velcro centered along the edge of the left front piece with the hooks facing outward and pin it in place. Sew around the Velcro, stitching close to the edge. Center the softer side (loop) of the Velcro along the inside edge of the right front piece, with the loops facing inward. Pin it in place. Ensure the two Velcro pieces are carefully aligned.

23
Sew around the Velcro as close as possible to the edge.

24
It should look like this when closed. Well done, the jacket is finished!

Tail-Fit Harem Pants

These harem pants are designed especially for raccoons, with a back opening to fit their tails just right. Stylish and easy to wear, they're made for dolls who need that little extra room!

CUTTING LAYOUT

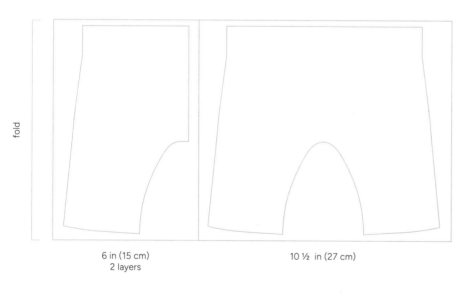

fold

6 in (15 cm)
2 layers

10 ½ in (27 cm)

9 in (23 cm)
selvedge

— **FABRIC**
A piece 22 ½ in (57 cm) wide x 9 in (23 cm) long

  Recommended fabric
  This pattern works well with cotton, linen, hemp or any light to medium-weight fabric

  SEWING THREAD
  100% polyester thread that matches the color of the fabric

  3/8 IN (1 CM) WIDE ELASTIC
  1 x 8 ¼ in (21 cm) long piece

  1/4 IN (0.6 CM) WIDE ELASTIC (optional)
  2 x 3 ½ in (9 cm) long pieces

— SAFETY PIN

— COTTON THREAD (optional)

— SEWING MACHINE

— SERGER (optional)

— FABRIC SCISSORS

— PINS

— IRON

TAIL-FIT HAREM PANTS

SEAM ALLOWANCE
⅜ in (0.9 cm) seam allowance included unless otherwise specified

1
Cut out the pattern pieces from the fabric following the grainline and take note of the markings (the small lines printed on the pattern pieces). You must have 1 front pants piece and 2 back pants pieces.

2
Place the two back pants pieces on top of the front pants piece with right sides together, pin and sew along each side.

3
Finish the seams using a serger or zigzag. Finish also the raw inner edges of both back pieces, as shown.

4
With right sides together, align the inner edges of the back pants pieces and sew as shown, leaving a 1 ½ in (4 cm) gap for the tail.

5
Press the seam allowances down on each side, and iron flat. Stitch onto each seam allowance to secure them on both sides.

6
It should look like this.

7
For gathered legs with an elastic casing, follow Steps 8-9. To hem the pants, fold the edge twice by ¼ in (0.6 cm) toward the inside, pin in place, and sew as close as possible to the folded edge.

8
For gathered legs, fold the bottom edge of each leg ¼ in (0.6 cm) toward the inside of fabric, then fold again 5/16 in (0.8 cm), pin in place, and sew along as close as possible to the folded edge. Cut out two 3 ½ in (9 cm) elastic pieces and using a safety pin, thread one through each casing.

9
Secure the elastic at both ends.

10
Repeat for both legs.

TAIL-FIT HAREM PANTS   81

11
With right sides of fabric facing, align the crotch and sew along the curved edge. Finish the seam.

12
Turn the pants right side out. To make the elastic casing for the waist, fold the fabric around the waistline ¼ in (0.6 cm) toward the inside of fabric, then fold again ½ in (1.2 cm) and pin in place. Use as many pins as possible.

13
Sew around the waistline, stitching as close as possible to the folded edge leaving a 1 in (2.5 cm) opening at the back to insert the elastic.

Cut out a 8 ¼ in (21 cm) long piece of ⅜ in (1 cm) wide elastic. Using a safety pin, thread the elastic through the waistline casing.

14
When the loose end of the elastic reaches the opening of the casing, pin it to hold it in place. Keep pushing the safety pin through the casing all the way around until both ends meet.

15
Overlap both ends of the elastic about ⅜ in (1 cm) and sew them together.

16
Sew along the waistline as shown to close the opening.

17
To finish, cut an 8 in (20 cm) piece of cotton thread and secure it to the center of the waistline at its midpoint.

Leave it loose or tie it into a bow as desired.

Voilà !

Suspender Pants

These suspender pants can be sewn as shorts, straight - leg pants, or wide-leg pants - giving you plenty of options to create the perfect look. Stylish and customizable, they're ready for any style you choose!

CUTTING LAYOUT

fold

10 in (26 cm) selvedge

11 ½ in (29 cm)
2 layers

— FABRIC
A piece 23 in (58 cm) wide x 10 in (26 cm) long

Recommended fabric
This pattern works well with cotton, hemp, linen or any light to medium-weight fabric.

— SCRAP FABRIC FOR MINI BOWS

— SEWING THREAD
100% polyester thread that matches the color of the fabric

— 2 DECORATIVE BUTTONS (optional)

— SEWING MACHINE

— SERGER (optional)

— FABRIC SCISSORS

— PINS

— IRON

SUSPENDER PANTS

SEAM ALLOWANCE
⅜ in (0.9 cm) seam allowance included
unless otherwise specified

1
Cut out the pattern pieces from the fabric following the grainline and take note of the markings (the small lines printed on the pattern pieces). You must have 2 suspenders, 2 front waistbands, 2 back waistbands, 2 ruffle pieces (optional) and depending on the style you choose, 2 shorts, or 2 straight or wide-leg pants pieces.

2
Start by sewing the darts. To do this, place one shorts or pants piece with the wrong side facing up. Fold one leg so the two dart markings align, with the right sides of the fabric together. Sew ¾ in (2 cm) along the fold, ⅜ in (0.9 cm) from the folded edge.

3
Do the same with the other piece. It should look like this on the right side of the fabric.

4
Place the two pieces with right sides together, pin and sew along the edges of fabric, as shown. Finish the seams.

5
Fold the bottom edge of both legs twice by ¼ in (0.6 cm) toward the inside of fabric. Pin in place. Sew along the bottom close to the folded edge.

6
With right sides facing, align the crotch, pin and sew along the curve. Finish the seam.

7
For the suspenders, start by folding them in half lengthwise and iron to mark the center. Then, fold both sides of each suspender inward toward the center so they meet in the middle. Iron to hold the folds in place.

8
To add ruffles to the suspenders, follow the steps below. If ruffles are not desired, skip to Step 15. Serger or zigzag stitch the curved edge of both ruffle pieces.

9
Fold the curved edge ¼ in (0.6 cm) toward the inside of the fabric, pin and sew close to the edge. Repeat for the other ruffle piece.

SUSPENDER PANTS 85

10
To create the ruffles, set the machine to the widest stitch possible and sew a basting stitch along the raw edge of both ruffle pieces at about ³⁄₁₆ in (0.5 cm) from the edge. Do not backstitch at either end and leave a few inches of thread before clipping.

11
Carefully pull on one of the threads to gather the fabric until the ruffle matches the distance between the two ruffle markings on the suspenders. (All markings are indicated on the pattern.)

12
Place each ruffle piece inside the suspenders, aligning them with the ruffle markings. Ensure the raw edge of the ruffle pieces is aligned with the center of the suspenders. Pin in place.

13
Sew to secure very close to the raw edge.

14
Fold the other half of the suspender over the ruffle edge and pin in place. Ensure both sides of the suspender are lined up, then sew along the open edge to secure the ruffle between the layers. Repeat for both suspenders.

15
Fold each suspender in half lengthwise and sew along the open edge close to the edge.

16
Lay one of the front waistband pieces in front of you with the right side facing up. Place both suspenders, right sides facing down, on the waistband, aligning them with the front suspender markings indicated on the pattern. Secure them in place by stitching close to the edge. If using ruffles, ensure they are facing outward.

17
Lay the second front waistband piece on top, with the right side facing the suspenders and the first waistband. Sew along the edge, as shown. Flip both waistbands so the right sides are facing out.

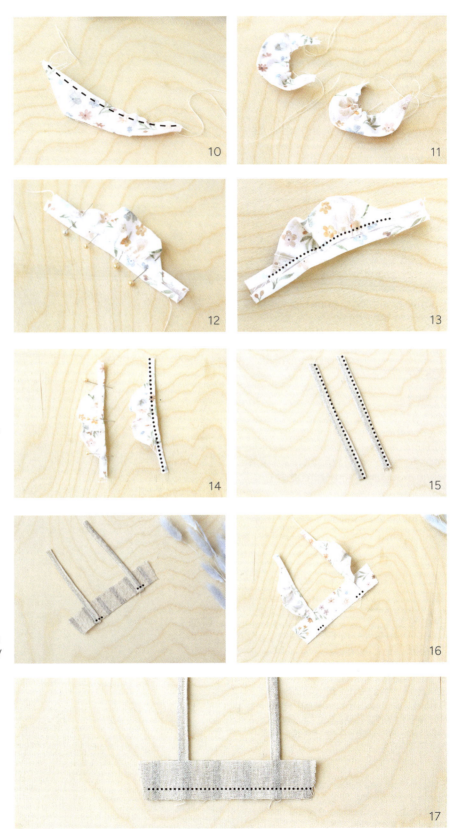

86 SUSPENDER PANTS

18
Lay one of the back waistband piece with the right side facing up. Cross the suspenders and align both ends with the suspender markings indicated on the pattern. Sew them in place.

19
Lay the second back waistband piece on top, with right side facing the suspenders Sew along the edge, as shown.

20
Flip both waistbands so the right sides are facing out and iron flat.

21
To sew the front and back waistbands together, align the sides of the front waistband with the sides of the back waisband, with right sides facing, and sew along the side edges, as shown.

22
Turn the assembled waistband right side out and iron flat.

23
With the shorts or pants turned inside out and the waistband right side out and upside down, insert the waistband into the garment.) The right sides of the fabric must be facing each other.)

24
Align raw edges and side seams, then pin all three layers of fabric together.

25
Sew around the waistline and finish the seam.

26
Turn the garment right side out.
You can hand-sew little buttons for a more dressed-up look.

27
Small bows can also be added to the front of the garment. (Refer to accordeon bow tutorial p. 94)

Beret

This French beret adds the perfect touch of charm to any outfit. Easy to slip on and style, it's the finishing accessory that'll make your doll look effortlessly chic!

CUTTING LAYOUT
MAIN FABRIC

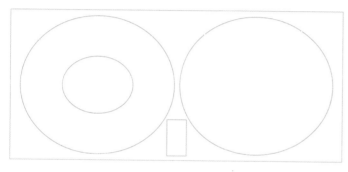

17 ½ in (45 cm)

LINING FABRIC

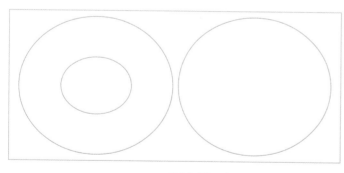

17 ½ in (45 cm)

— **FABRIC**
A piece 17 ½ in (45 cm) wide x 8 in (20 cm) long for both the main fabric and lining.

Recommended fabric
This pattern works well with medium to heavy-weight fabrics, such as wool felt, tweed, or flannel, for the main fabric, and cotton or flannel for the lining.

— **SEWING THREAD**
100% polyester thread that matches the color of the fabric

— **FABRIC SCISSORS**

— **SEWING MACHINE**

— **PINS**

— **IRON**

90 BERET

SEAM ALLOWANCE
⅜ in (0.9 cm) seam allowance included unless otherwise specified

1
Cut out the pattern pieces from the fabric following the grainline and take note of the markings (the small lines printed on the pattern pieces). You must have 2 upper piece, 2 lower piece and 1 stem piece.

2
With right sides together, pin the main fabric lower piece with the main fabric upper piece, aligning edges. Sew all around the outer edge with a ³⁄₁₆ in (0.5 cm) seam allowance.

3
Repeat Step 2 with the lining pieces. Trim the seam allowance using pinking shears or by making small triangle cuts.

4
Turn the lining of the beret right side out and iron the seams flat.

5
Insert the lining into the main fabric piece, with the right sides facing each other. Align the center markings of both the lining and the main fabric.

6
Pin and sew the pieces together by stitching along the inner edge, leaving a 2 in (5 cm) opening for turning.

7
Turn the beret right side out through the opening. Using a chopstick, press the inside seams to create a smooth curve and iron the seams flat.

8
Pin the opening closed.

9
Topstitch all around the inner circle (bottom of the beret) close to the edge going over the gap opening to close it.

10
Fold both short ends of the stem piece toward the wrong side of the fabric and iron. Then, fold both long sides of the stem piece lengthwise so they meet at the center and iron.

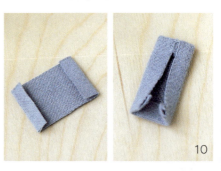

BERET 91

11
Fold the stem in half lengthwise, aligning the two folded edges and pin in place. Sew along the open edges stitching very close to the edge.

12
To attach the stem to the beret, begin by threading the needle with both ends of a folded thread. Fold the stem in half widthwise, and tie the thread to one end of the stem using the knotless start (refer p.8). Sew the two ends of the stem together using the ladder stitch by inserting the needle along the edges from one side to the other until reaching the opposite end. Do not cut the thread.

13
Fold the beret in half lengthwise, then fold it in half widthwise to locate the center. The tip of the cone formed by these folds is the center of the circle. Mark this point with an erasable fabric pen.

14
Pin the stem to the center of the beret on the right side of the fabric.

15
Using the same thread, pass the needle through the beret fabric and then through the stem, repeating this all around until the stem is firmly attached.

16
Finish with a slip knot. (Refer p.9)

17
Complete the look by dressing up your doll with this chic, fashionable beret!

17

Accordion Bow/Bow Tie

This bow (or bow tie) is the sweetest finishing touch! Whether tied neat or playful, it adds a little extra charm to any outfit - perfect for a doll who loves to stand out!

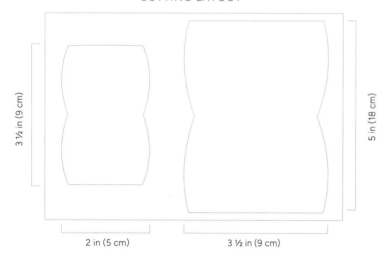

CUTTING LAYOUT

- **FABRIC**
  A piece 3 ½ in (9 cm) wide
  x 5 in (18 cm) long for the regular size bow

  A piece 2 in (5 cm) wide
  x 3 ½ in (9 cm) long for the mini bow

  Recommended fabric
  This pattern works well with any light-weight fabric.

- **SEWING THREAD**
  100% polyester thread that matches the color of the fabrics

- **SEWING MACHINE**

- **HANDSEWING NEEDLE**

- **FABRIC SCISSORS**

- **PINS**

94 ACCORDION BOW/BOW TIE

SEAM ALLOWANCE
⅜ in (0.9 cm) seam allowance included
unless otherwise specified

1
Cut out the pattern piece from the fabric following the grainline. You can choose from two sizes: Regular or Mini.

2
With right sides together, fold the fabric in half widthwise. Sew along the edges, leaving a 1 in (2.5 cm) opening at the bottom, as shown.

3
Turn the bow right side out and iron flat. Hand-sew the opening closed using the ladder stitch. (Refer p.9)

4
To create the folds, start by folding the top of the fabric in half. Continue folding in the same direction, layering the fabric, until reaching the bottom edge. This will create an accordion-style fold for the bow.

To gather the center of the bow, thread the needle with both ends of a long folded thread. (This thread will be used both to gather the center and to attach the bow to the doll). Start at the top center of the bow and push the needle through all layers, bringing it out at the bottom.

5
Then, from the bottom, push the needle back through all layers, positioning it close to the previous stitch, and bring it out at the top. Pass the needle through the loop formed at the top, and pull the thread tight to secure the gather.

6
Wrap the thread tightly around the center three or four times, then secure it with a slip knot. Do not cut the remaining thread.

7
Attach the bow or bow tie to your favorite doll.

96   ACCESSORIES

Pinwheel Bow

This dainty bow adds a hint of sweetness wherever it goes. With its soft curves and delicate charm, it brings a playful pop to any look!

CUTTING LAYOUT

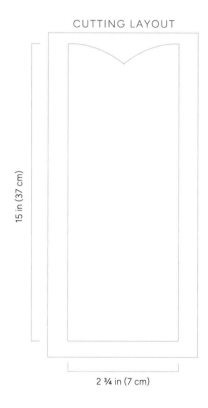

15 in (37 cm)

2 ¾ in (7 cm)

— **FABRIC**
A piece 2 ¾ in (7 cm) wide
x 15 in (37 cm) long

Recommended fabric
This pattern works well with
any light-weight fabric.

— **SEWING THREAD**
100% polyester thread that matches
the color of the fabric

— HAND SEWING NEEDLE

— SEWING MACHINE

— FABRIC SCISSORS

— PINS

98　PINWHEEL BOW

SEAM ALLOWANCE
⅜ in (0.9 cm) seam allowance included unless otherwise specified

1
Cut out the pattern piece from folded fabric, following the grainline.

2
Fold the piece of fabric in half lengthwise with the right sides facing each other.

Sew along all three edges, leaving a 1 in (2.5 cm) opening at the center.

3
Turn the piece right side out using a loop turner or a chopstick.

4
Iron flat, positionning the seams at the sides. Hand-sew the opening closed using the ladder stitch. (Refer p.9)

Alternatively, close the opening by machine sewing close to the edge.

5
To create the bow, begin by folding the fabric in half widthwise, aligning the two ends.

6
While keeping the fabric folded, fold each end inward toward the center, forming two loops.

7
Then, cross one loop over the other and tuck it underneath.

8
Finally, pull the loops tight to secure the bow.

9
Adjust the bow by rearranging the loops, evenly distributing the fabric folds, and gently pulling the loops until the desired shape is achieved.

Mini Maddy Jumpsuit/Dress

This mini Maddy offers both charm and versatility - it can be sewn as a dress or a jumpsuit, letting style take the lead. With a ribbon at the neck for an easy fit, it's a playful piece ready for any adventure.

CUTTING LAYOUT
JUMPSUIT OPTION

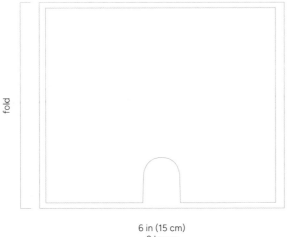

6 in (15 cm)
2 layers

- FABRIC
  A piece 12 in (30 cm) wide x 5 in (13 cm) long for the jumpsuit

  A piece 12 in (30 cm) wide x 4 in (10 cm) long for the dress

  Recommended fabric
  This pattern works well with cotton, linen, hemp or any light-weight fabrics.

- SEWING THREAD
  100% polyester thread that matches the color of the fabric

- RIBBON OR ANY THIN FABRIC TRIM
  1 x 13 in (32 cm) long piece

- 1/4 IN ELASTIC (optional)
  2 x 3 in (7.5 cm) long pieces

- SAFETY PIN

- SEWING MACHINE

- SERGER (optional)

- FABRIC SCISSORS

- PINS

- RULER

- IRON

MINI MADDY JUMPSUIT/DRESS

SEAM ALLOWANCE
⅜ in (0.9 cm) seam allowance included unless otherwise specified

1
Cut out the pattern pieces from the fabric following the grainline and take note of the markings (the small lines printed on the pattern pieces). You must have, depending on the style you choose, 2 dress pieces or 2 jumpsuit pieces. No matter the chosen style, the steps to follow are the same except otherwise indicated.

2
Using a serger or a zigzag stitch on a regular machine, finish both side edges of each piece of the garment (front and back), to prevent fraying.

3
Place the two pieces right sides together, aligning edges and pin in place.

Sew along both sides from the armhole markings to the bottom, as shown. (All markings are indicated on the pattern.)

4
Press the seam allowances down on each side, and iron flat.

Sew along the armhole as shown to secure the seam allowances down both sides.

5
To create the casing for the ribbon, fold the top edge of each piece (front and back) ¼ in (0.6 cm) toward the inside of fabric. Then, fold again 5⁄16 in (0.8 cm), iron and pin in place. The folds should align with the neckline markings indicated on the pattern.

6
Sew along the edge as shown, as close as possible to the folded edge, on both pieces.

7
This is an other view of the folded top edges (casings).

8
It should look like this at this point.

MINI MADDY JUMPSUIT/DRESS   103

9
For the jumpsuit with gathered legs, skip to Step 10. For a simple hem, fold the bottom edge of the dress or each leg of the jumpsuit twice by ¼ in (0.6 cm) toward the inside of fabric, and pin in place. Sew along the bottom as close as possible to the folded edge.

10
To make the elastic casing for the gathered legs, fold the bottom edge of each leg ¼ in (0.6 cm) toward the inside of the fabric, fold again 5⁄16 in (0.8 cm), and pin in place. Sew along the bottom edges as close as possible to the folded edge.

Cut two 3 in (7.5 cm) long pieces of ¼ in (0.6 cm) wide elastic. Using a safety pin, thread one elastic through each casing.

11
When the loose end of the elastic reaches the edge of the casing, secure it in place by sewing a couple of back and forth stitches along the edge. Keep pushing the safety pin through the casing and secure it at the other end also. Repeat for both legs.

12
For the jumpsuit, whether using elastic or not, align the crotch edges with the right sides of fabric facing each other, and pin in place.

Sew along the curved edge and finish the seam.

13
Turn the garment right side out.

14
Using a safety pin, thread the ribbon through the neck casing of both the front and back of the garment, then tie it into a bow.

Bravo !

Mini Skirt & Ruffle Collar

Soft and charming, this mini skirt and ruffle collar create a sweet, girly look. A perfect pair for mixing, matching, and dressing up with ease!

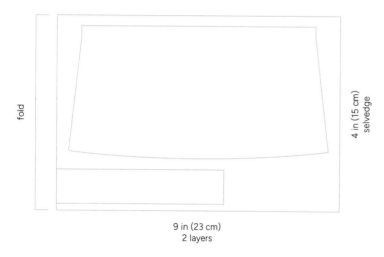

CUTTING LAYOUT
SKIRT OPTION

fold

4 in (15 cm) selvedge

9 in (23 cm)
2 layers

- **FABRIC**
  Skirt:
  A piece 18 in (46 cm) wide x 4 in (10 cm) long
  Collar:
  A piece 12 in (30 cm) wide x 2 in (5 cm) long

  Recommended fabric
  This pattern works well with cotton, double gauze, linen or any light to medium-weight fabric.

- **SEWING THREAD**
  100% polyester thread that matches the color of the fabric

- **¼ IN (0.6 CM) WIDE ELASTIC**
  1 x 5 in (12 cm) piece long
  1 x 6 in (15 cm) piece long

- SAFETY PIN
- SEWING MACHINE
- SERGER (optional)
- FABRIC SCISSORS
- PINS
- IRON

MINI SKIRT AND RUFFLE COLLAR

SEAM ALLOWANCE
⅜ in (0.9 cm) seam allowance included unless otherwise specified

1
For the skirt, cut out the pattern pieces from the fabric following the grainline. You must have 2 skirt pieces.

2
Place the two skirt pieces with right sides together, aligning the side edges and pin in place. Sew along one side as shown. Finish the seam using a serger or a zigzag stitch.

3
Finish the entire top edge of the assembled piece with a serger or a zigzag stitch. (The straight edge of the skirt is the top edge (waist) and the slightly curved edge is the bottom.)

4
To make the elastic casing, fold the top edge 5⁄16 in (0.8 cm) toward the inside of the fabric and pin in place. Sew as shown, stitching close to the edge of fabric.

5
Cut out a 5 in (13 cm) long piece of ¼ in (0.6 cm) wide elastic. Using a safety pin, thread the elastic through the casing.

6
When the loose end of the elastic reaches the edge of the casing, secure it in place by sewing a few back and forth stitches along the edge. Keep pushing the safety pin through the casing and secure it at the other end also.

7
Fold the skirt in half with right sides facing, aligning side edges. Pin and sew along the edge as shown. Finish the seam using a serger or a zigzag stitch.

8
Turn the skirt right side out. To hem the bottom, fold the edge twice by ¼ in (0.6 cm) toward the inside, iron and pin. Sew all around, stitching as close as possible to the folded edge.

9
Voilà.

MINI SKIRT AND RUFFLE COLLAR 107

1
Cut a 12 in (30 cm) wide × 2 in (5 cm) long rectangle from the fabric. (No pattern piece is provided for this.)

Fold the fabric piece in half lengthwise and pin in place. Sew along the raw edge of the fabric starting and stopping the seam 1 in (2.5 cm) from the beginning and end of the fabric.

2
Turn the tube halfway right side out, aligning both ends. To do this, attach a safety pin to one end of the tube and thread it through the inside until both ends meet.

3
Align the seams and the edges. Sew the ends together, stitching along the raw edges.

4
Turn the tube right side out through the seam gap and iron flat, positioning the seam along one side. Cut out one 6 in (15 cm) long piece of ¼ in (0.6 cm) wide elastic.

Attach a safety pin to one end of the elastic and thread it through the tube using the opening on the side.

5
When the loose end of the elastic reaches the opening of the tube, pin it to hold it in place. Keep pushing the safety pin through the tube all the way around until both ends meet.

6
Tie the two ends together securely and pull the knot tight.

7
Align and pin the two folded edges of the opening together. Close the opening by stitching as close as possible to the edge.

Templates

SEAM ALLOWANCE
⅜ in (0.9 cm) seam allowance included unless otherwise specified

--- Cut along the dashed line

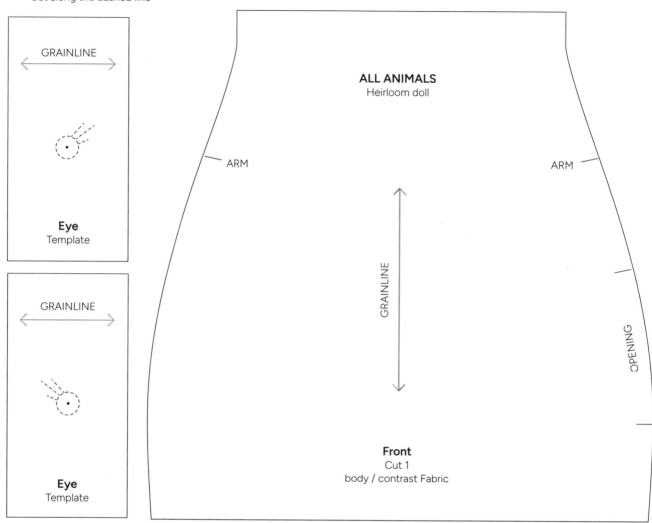

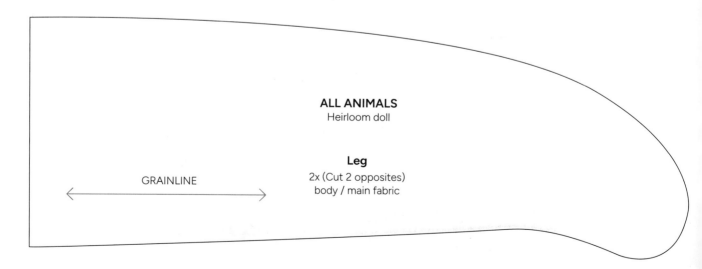

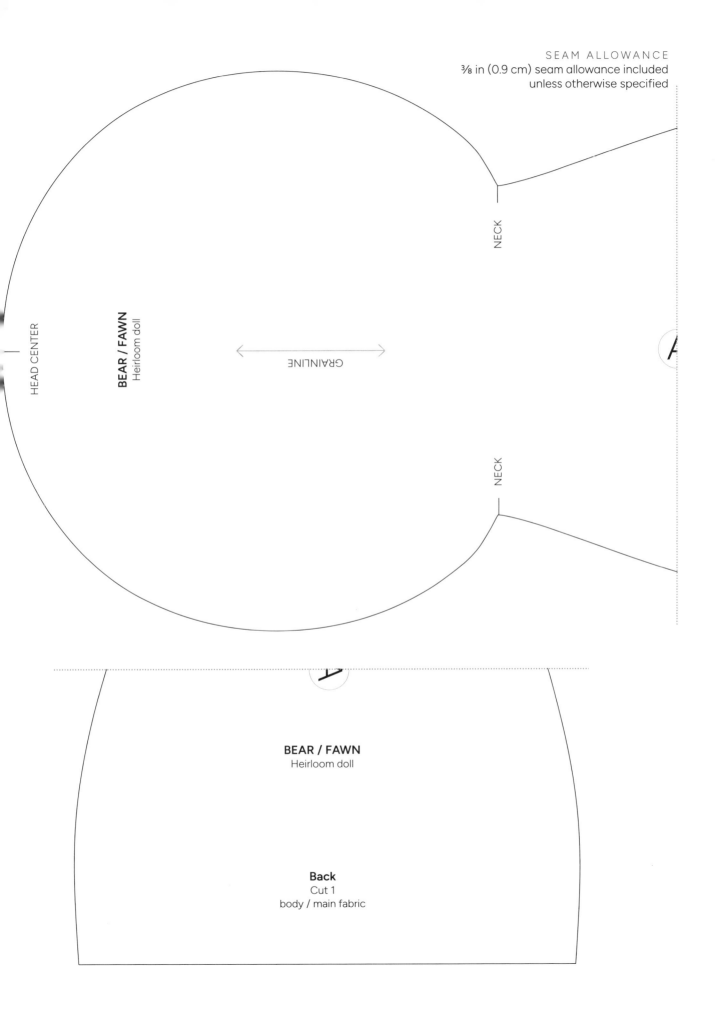

SEAM ALLOWANCE
⅜ in (0.9 cm) seam allowance included unless otherwise specified

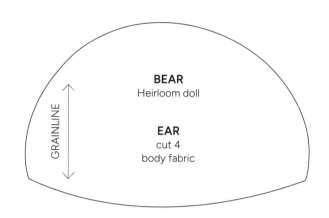
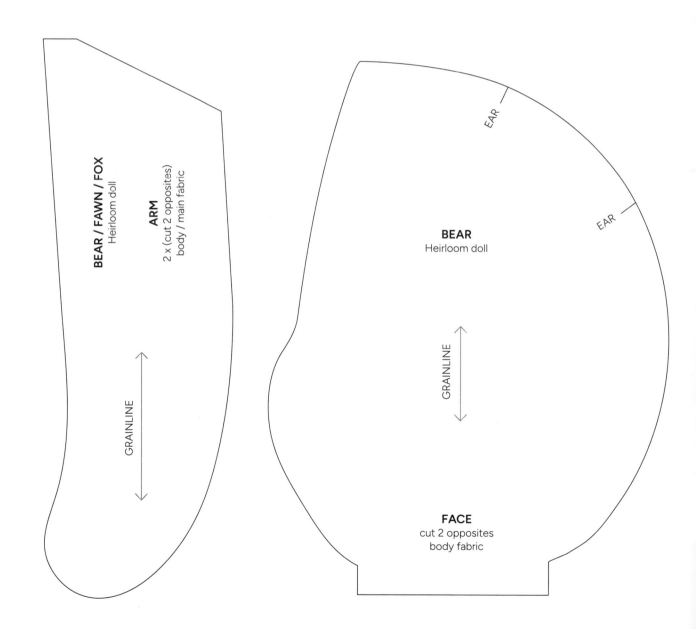

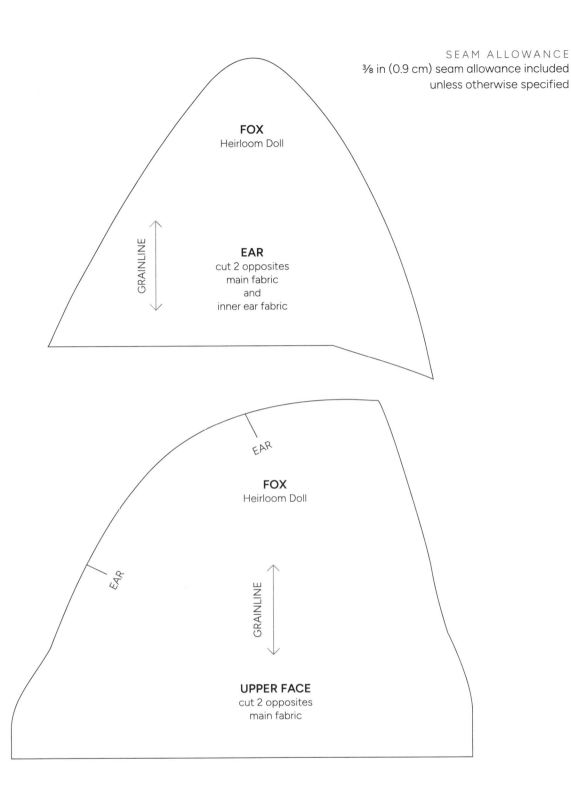

SEAM ALLOWANCE
⅜ in (0.9 cm) seam allowance included unless otherwise specified

--- Cut along the dashed line

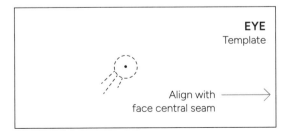

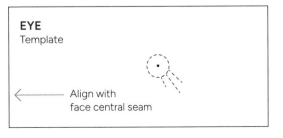

SEAM ALLOWANCE
⅜ in (0.9 cm) seam allowance included
unless otherwise specified

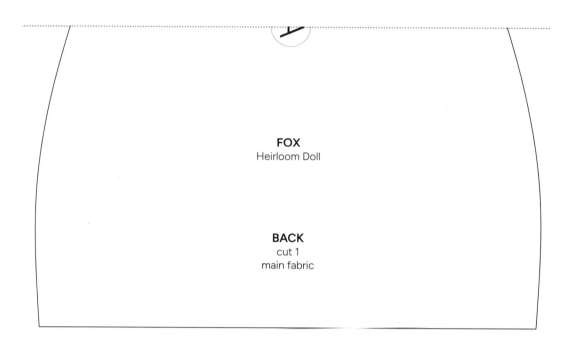

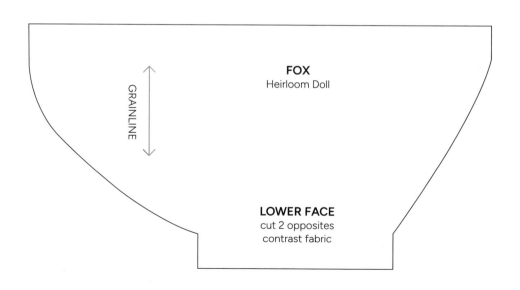

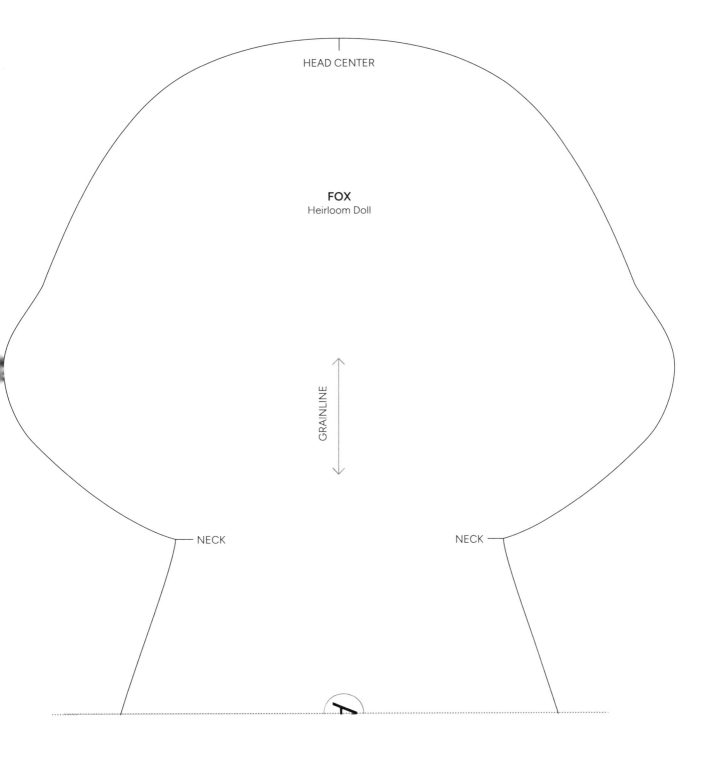

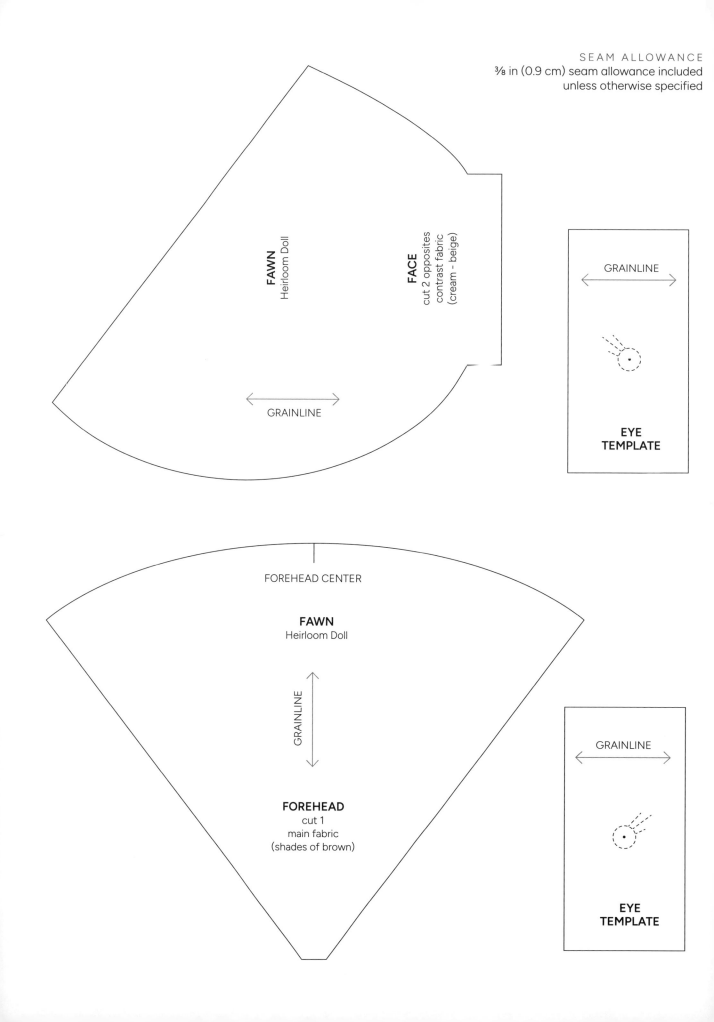

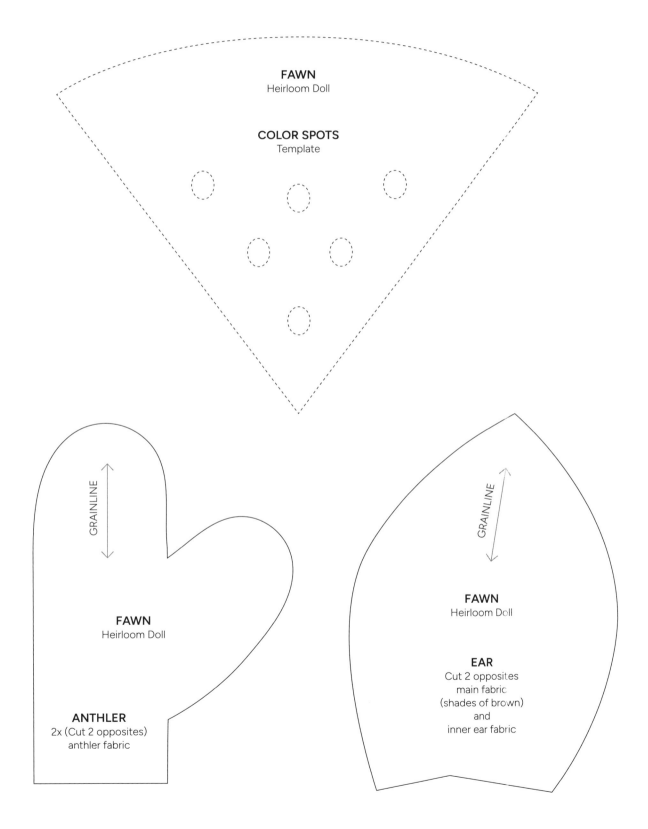

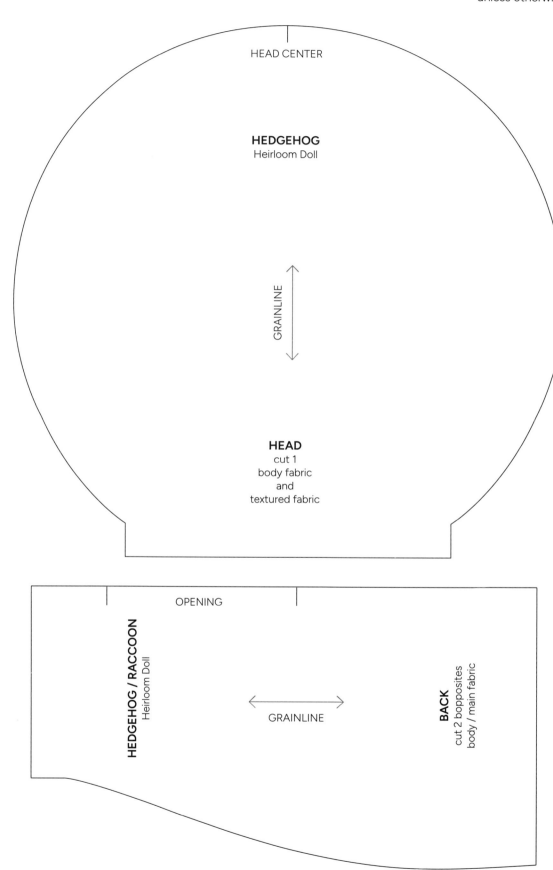

SEAM ALLOWANCE
⅜ in (0.9 cm) seam allowance included
unless otherwise specified

HEDGEHOG
Heirloom Doll

GRAINLINE

FOREHEAD
cut 2 opposites
body fabric
and
textured fabric

**HEDGEHOG /
RACCOON**
Heirloom Doll

GRAINLINE

ARM
2x (cut 2 opposites)
body / main fabric

HEDGEHOG
Heirloom Doll

GRAINLINE

HEDGEHOG
Heirloom Doll

GRAINLINE

EAR
2x (cut 2 opposites)
body fabric
and
inner ear fabric

EAR

LOWER FACE
cut 2 opposites
body fabric

SEAM ALLOWANCE
⅜ in (0.9 cm) seam allowance included
unless otherwise specified

HEAD CENTER

RACCOON
Heirloom Doll

GRAINLINE

BACK HEAD
cut 1
main fabric

RACCOON
Heirloom Doll

GRAINLINE

EYE PATCH
cut 2 opposites
felt fabric

RACCOON
Heirloom Doll

GRAINLINE

EAR
cut 2
main fabric
and
inner ear fabric

SEAM ALLOWANCE
⅜ in (0.9 cm) seam allowance included
unless otherwise specified

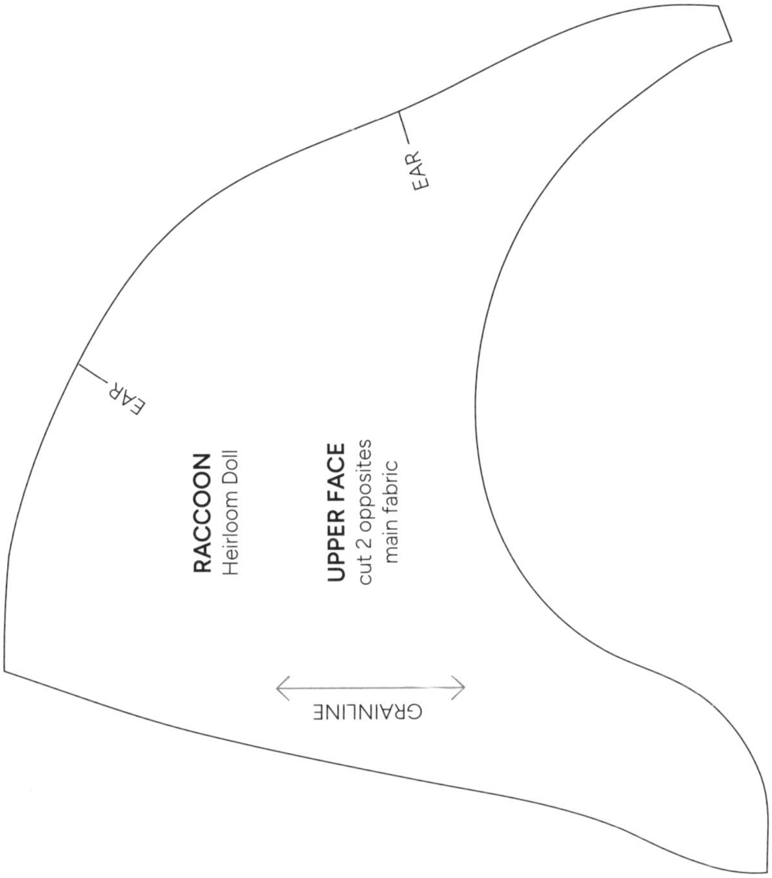

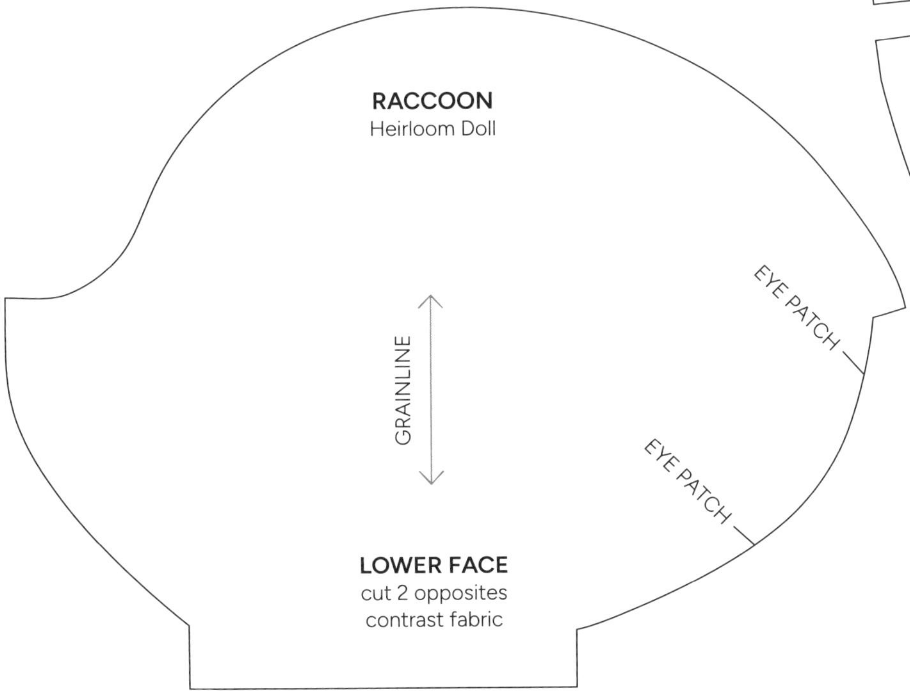

EAR

EAR

RACCOON
Heirloom Doll

UPPER FACE
cut 2 opposites
main fabric

GRAINLINE

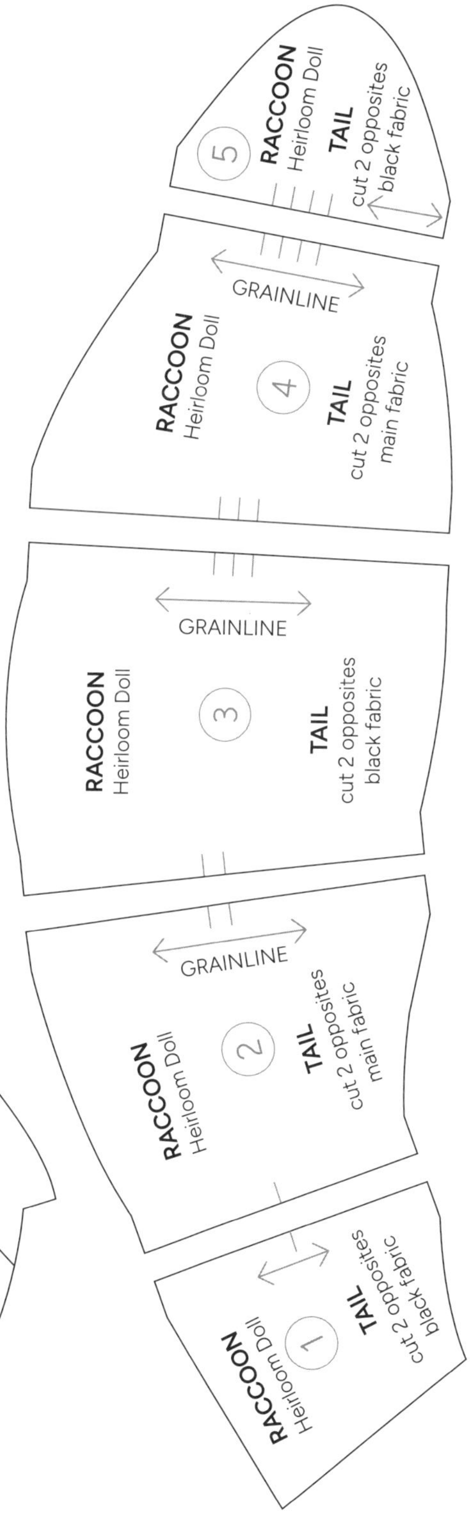

RACCOON
Heirloom Doll

GRAINLINE

EYE PATCH

EYE PATCH

LOWER FACE
cut 2 opposites
contrast fabric

RACCOON
Heirloom Doll

TAIL
cut 2 opposites
black fabric

⑤

RACCOON
Heirloom Doll

GRAINLINE

TAIL
cut 2 opposites
main fabric

④

RACCOON
Heirloom Doll

GRAINLINE

TAIL
cut 2 opposites
black fabric

③

RACCOON
Heirloom Doll

GRAINLINE

TAIL
cut 2 opposites
main fabric

②

RACCOON
Heirloom Doll

TAIL
cut 2 opposites
black fabric

①

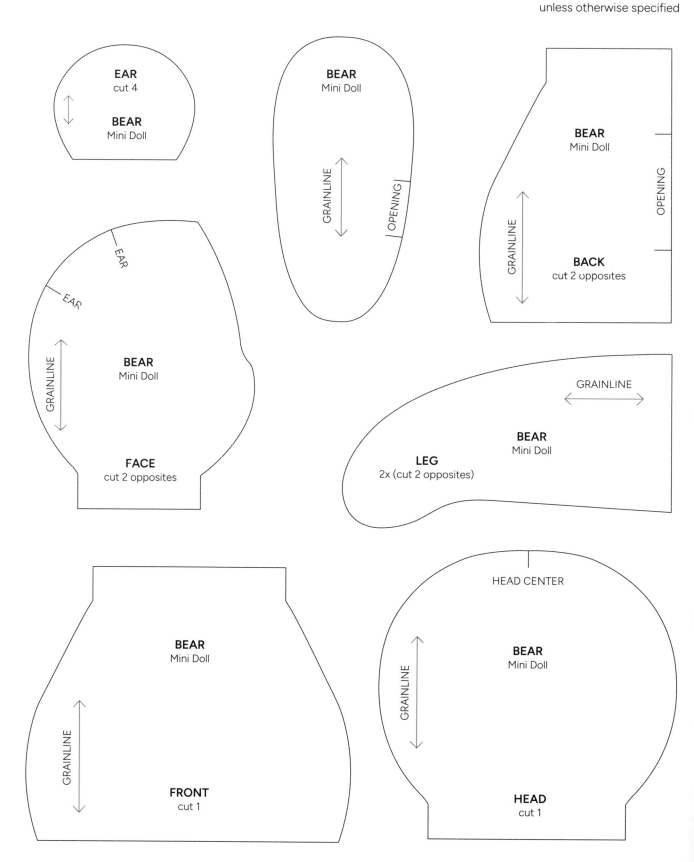

SEAM ALLOWANCE
⅜ in (0.9 cm) seam allowance included
unless otherwise specified

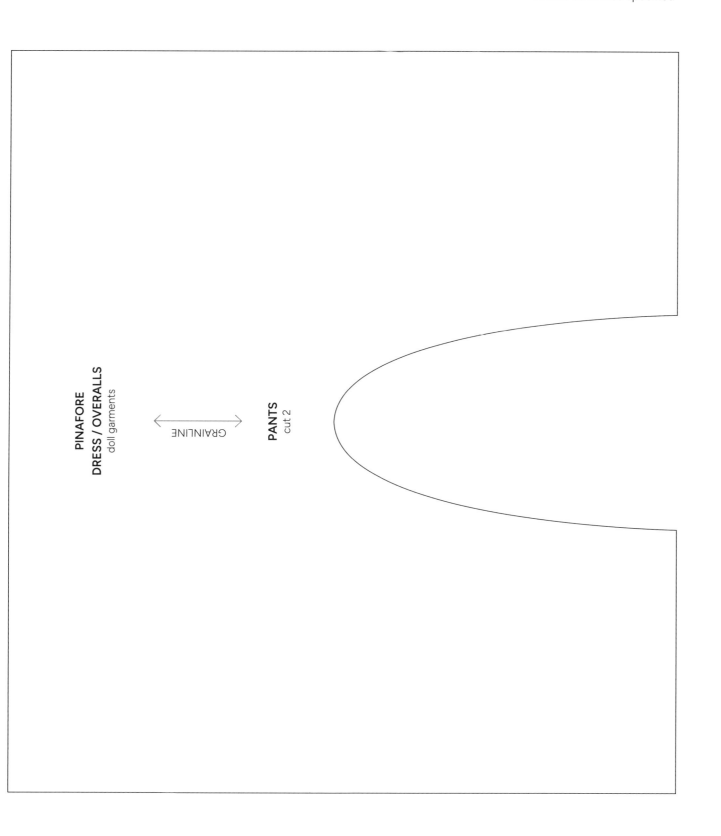

SEAM ALLOWANCE
⅜ in (0.9 cm) seam allowance included
unless otherwise specified

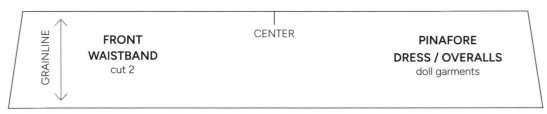
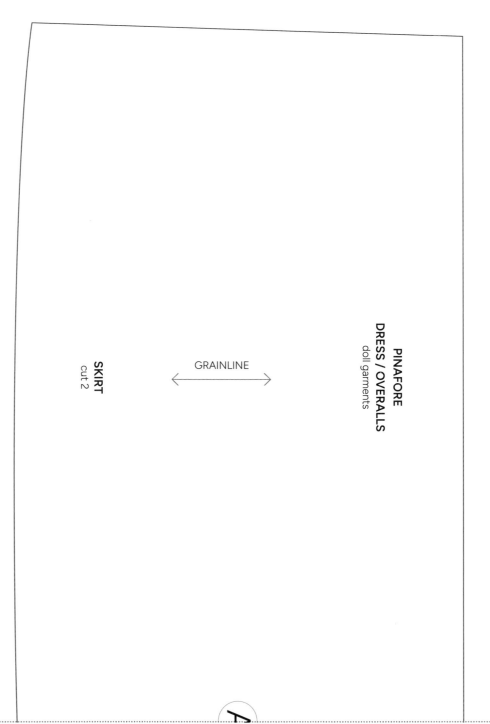

SEAM ALLOWANCE
⅜ in (0.9 cm) seam allowance included
unless otherwise specified

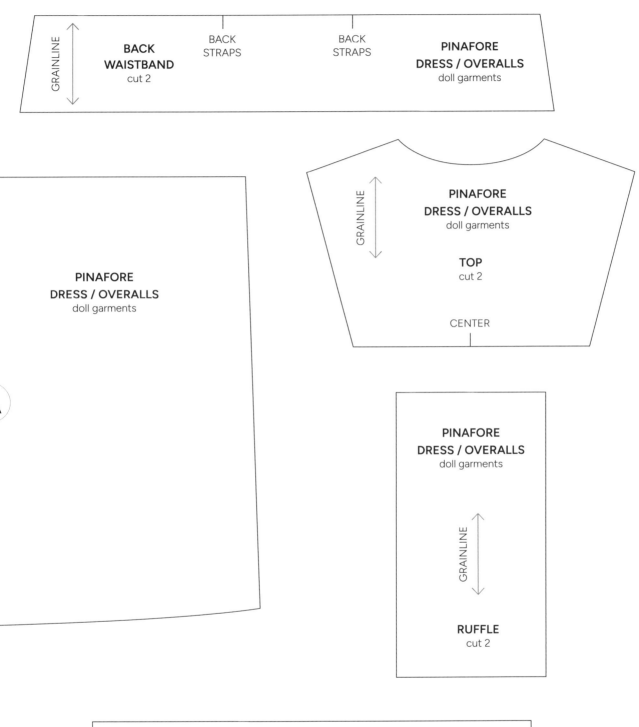

SEAM ALLOWANCE
⅜ in (0.9 cm) seam allowance included
unless otherwise specified

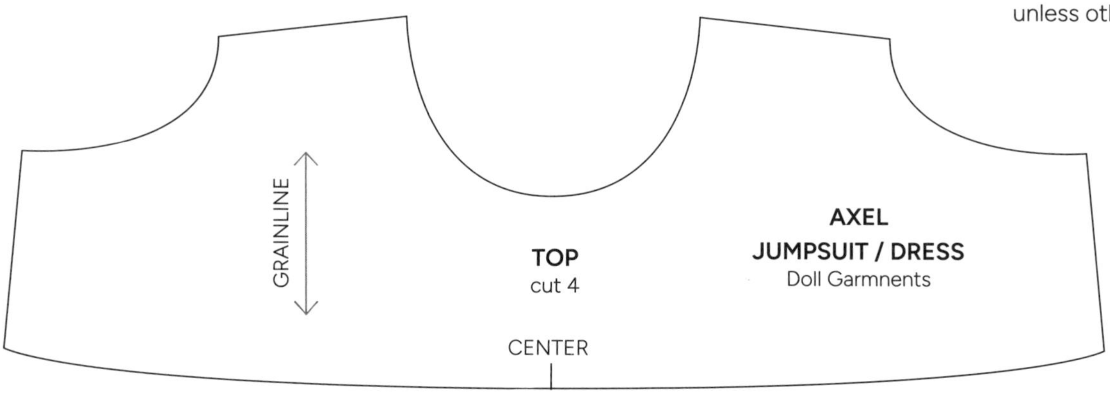

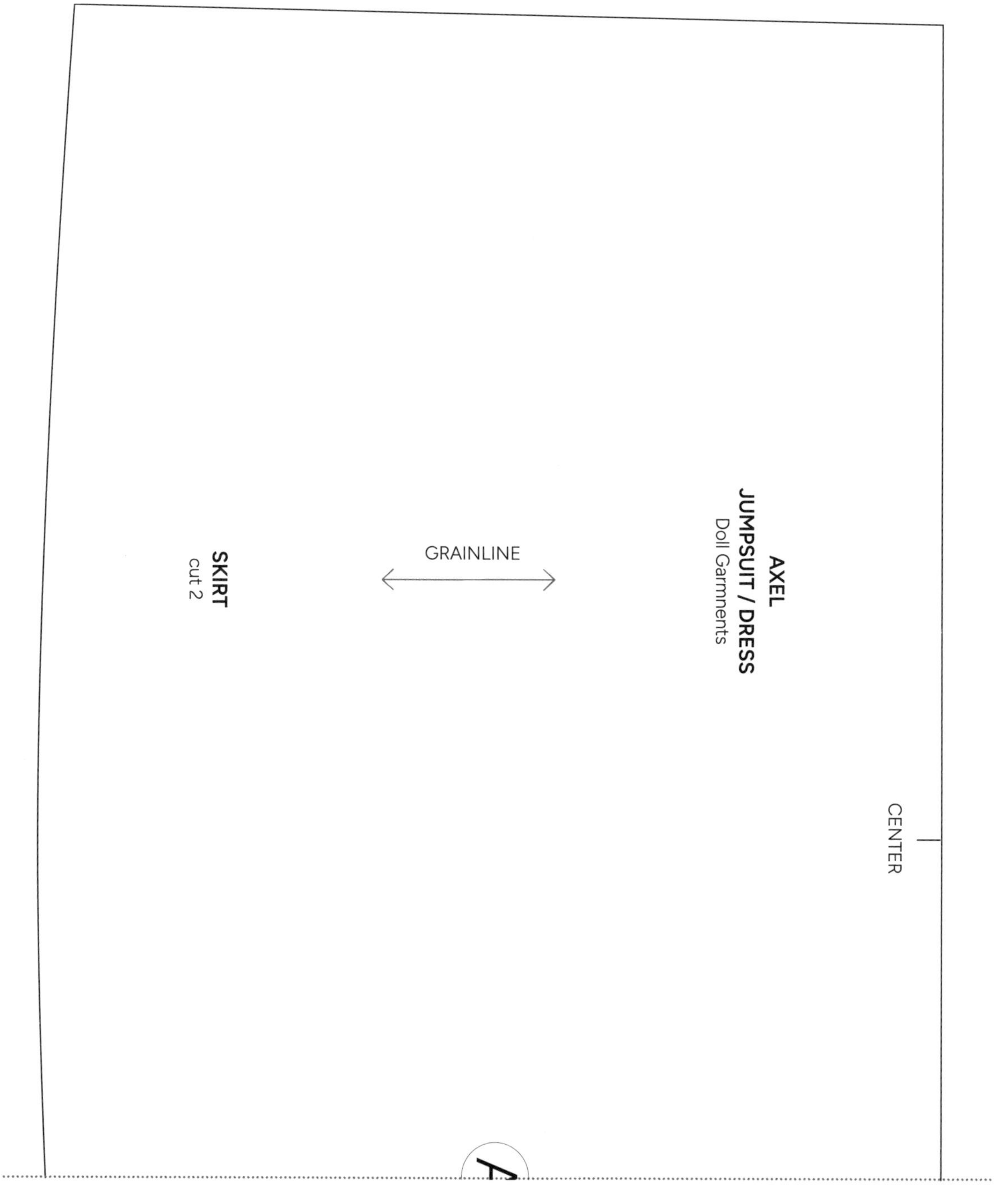

GRAINLINE

TOP
cut 4

AXEL
JUMPSUIT / DRESS
Doll Garmnents

CENTER

GRAINLINE

SKIRT
cut 2

AXEL
JUMPSUIT / DRESS
Doll Garmnents

CENTER

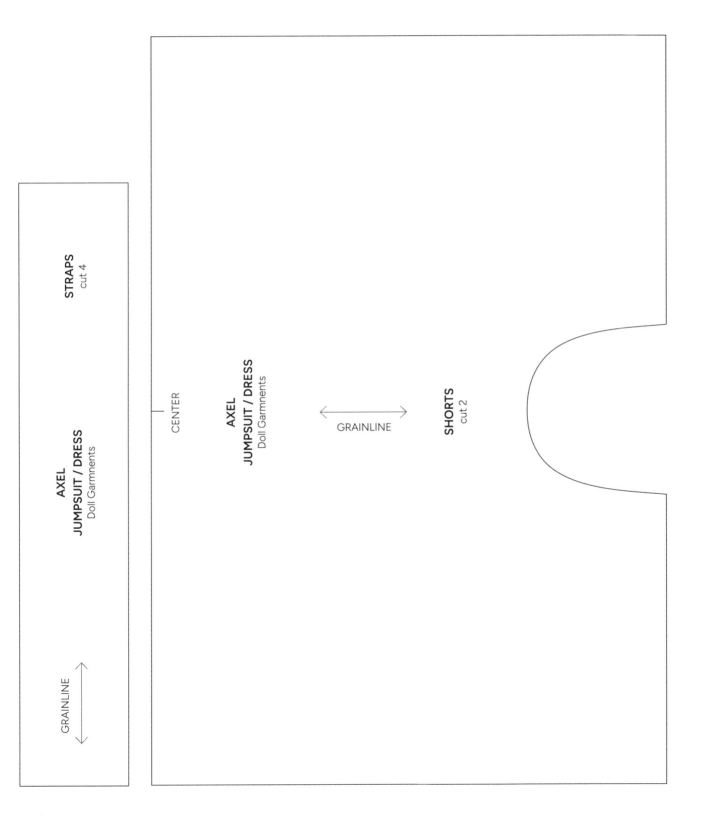

SEAM ALLOWANCE
⅜ in (0.9 cm) seam allowance included
unless otherwise specified

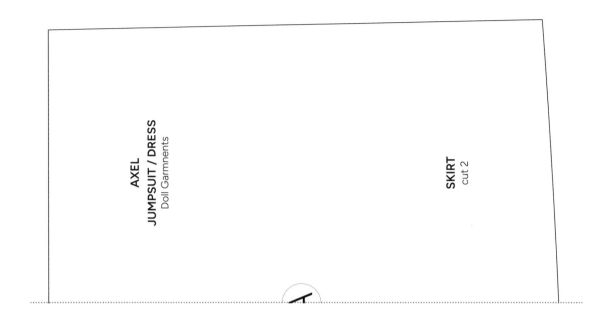

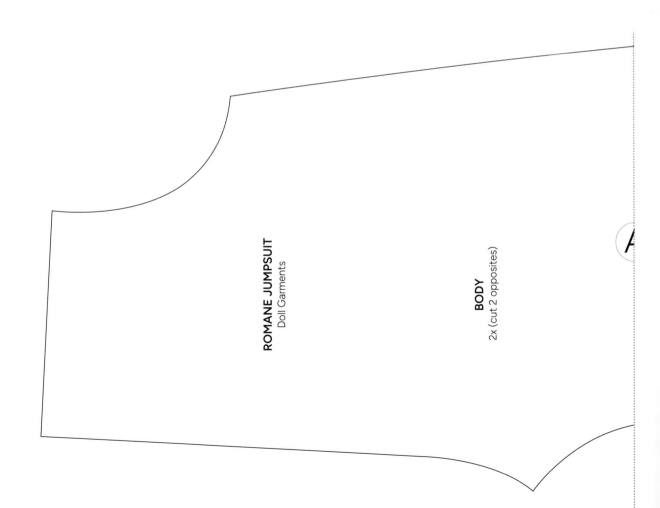

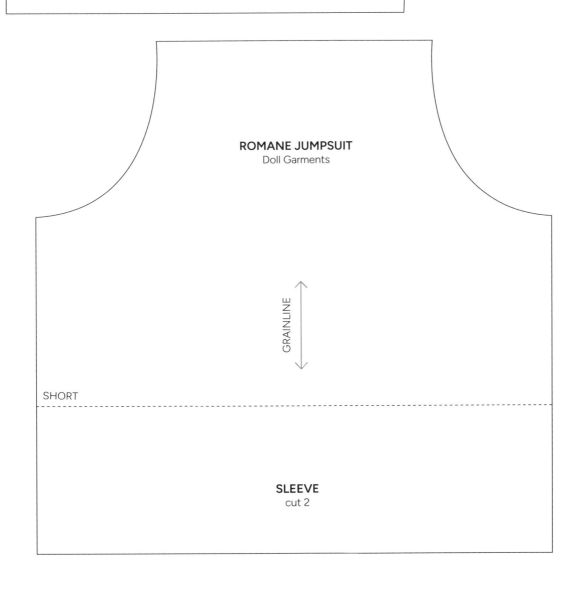

SEAM ALLOWANCE
⅜ in (0.9 cm) seam allowance included unless otherwise specified

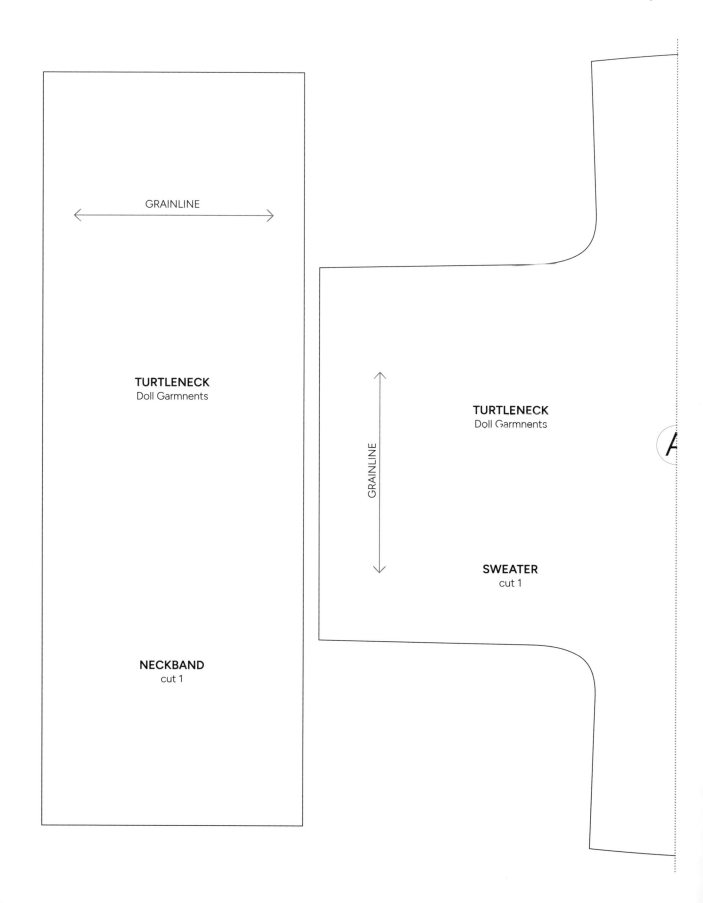

SEAM ALLOWANCE
⅜ in (0.9 cm) seam allowance included
unless otherwise specified

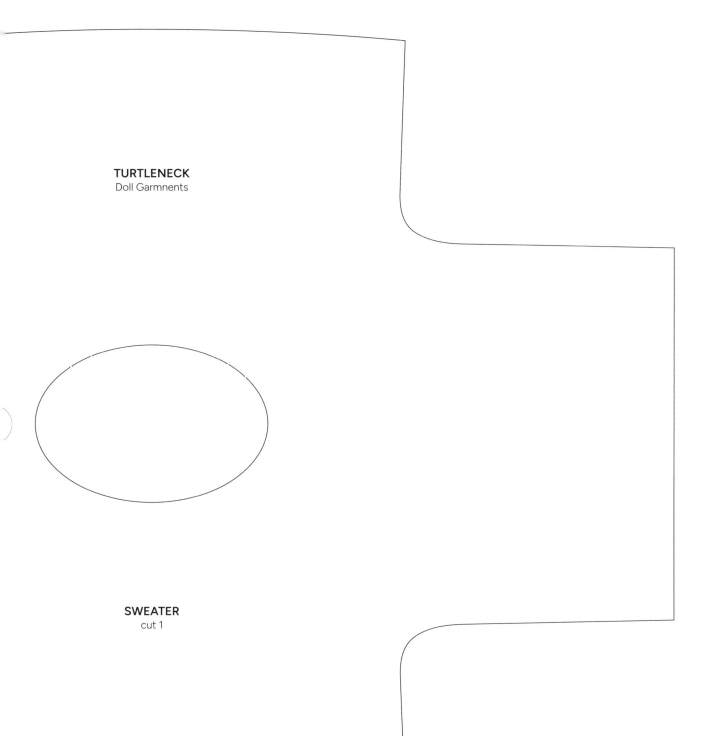

TURTLENECK
Doll Garmnents

SWEATER
cut 1

SEAM ALLOWANCE
⅜ in (0.9 cm) seam allowance included
unless otherwise specified

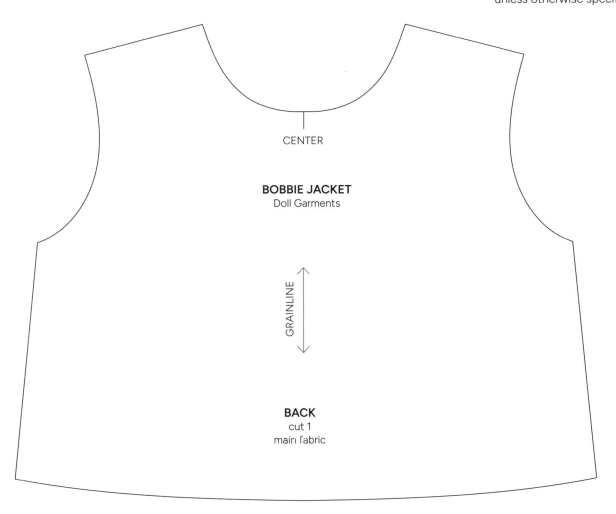

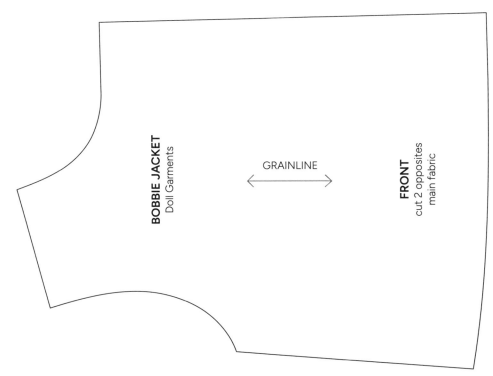

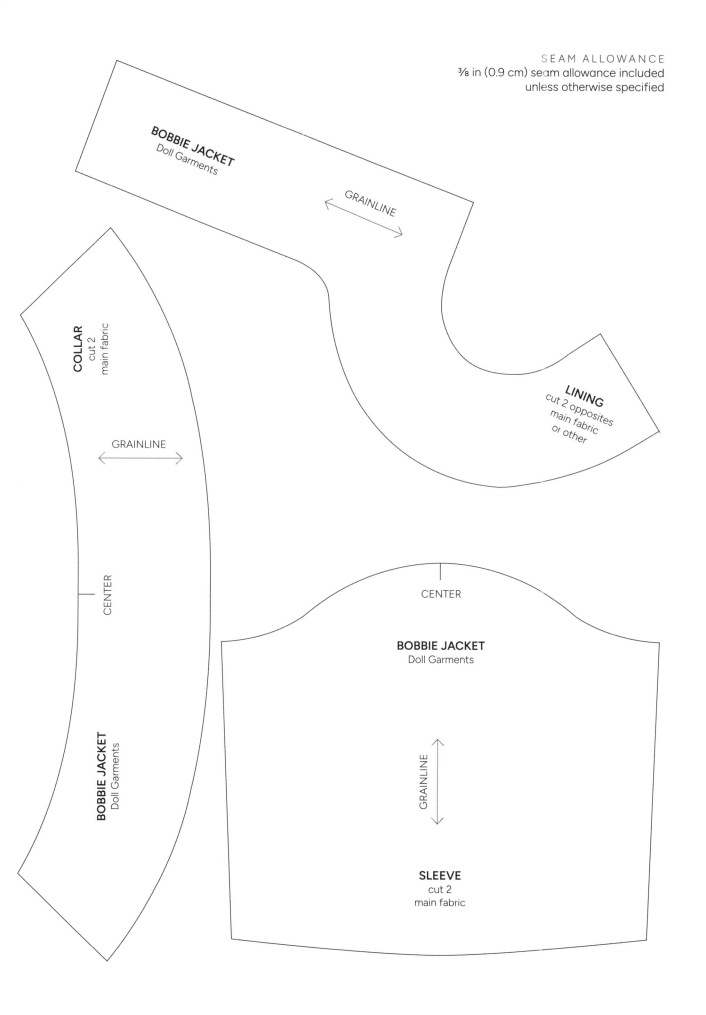

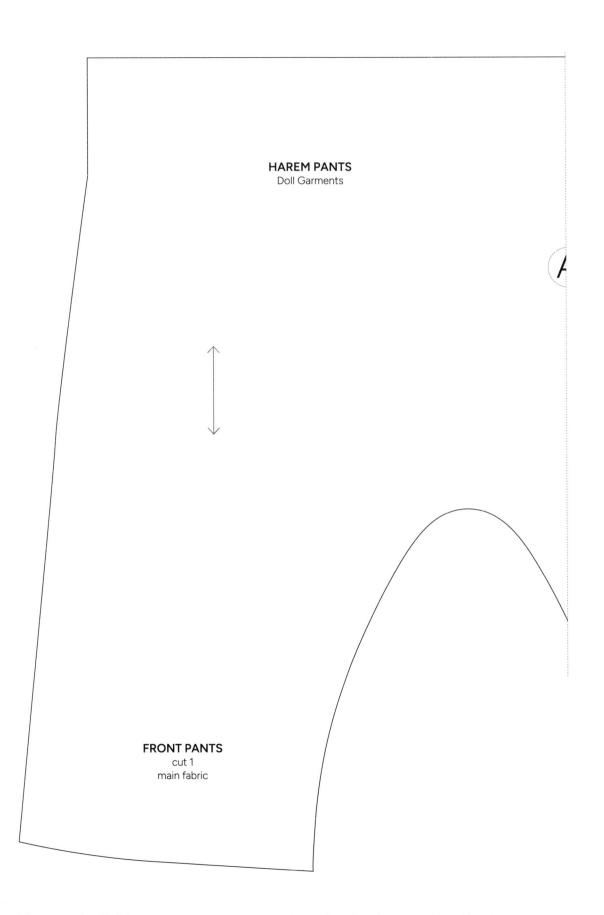

SEAM ALLOWANCE
³⁄₈ in (0.9 cm) seam allowance included
unless otherwise specified

SEAM ALLOWANCE
⅜ in (0.9 cm) seam allowance included
unless otherwise specified

HAREM PANTS
Doll Garments

A

FRONT PANTS
cut 1
main fabric

SEAM ALLOWANCE
⅜ in (0.9 cm) seam allowance included
unless otherwise specified

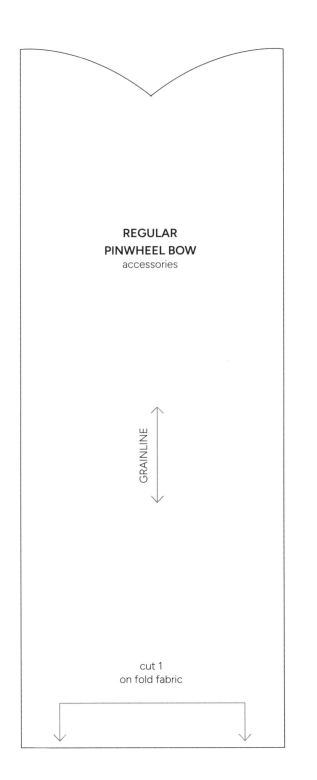
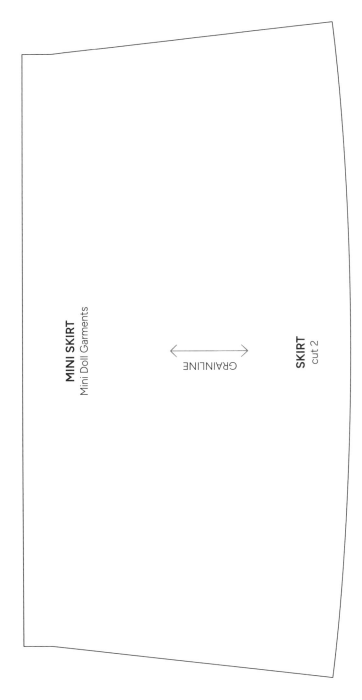

SEAM ALLOWANCE
⅜ in (0.9 cm) seam allowance included
unless otherwise specified

SUSPENDER PANTS
Doll Garments

RUFFLE
cut 2

GRAINLINE

DART

DART

SUSPENDER PANTS
Doll Garments

GRAINLINE

SHORTS
cut 2

STRAIGHT PANTS
cut 2

SEAM ALLOWANCE
⅜ in (0.9 cm) seam allowance included
unless otherwise specified

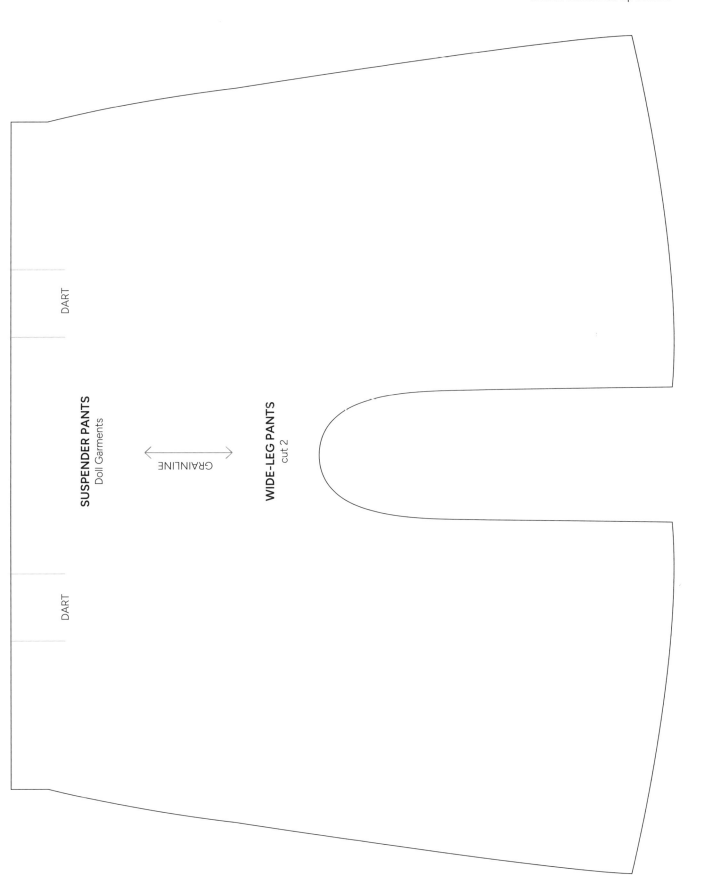

SEAM ALLOWANCE
⅜ in (0.9 cm) seam allowance included
unless otherwise specified

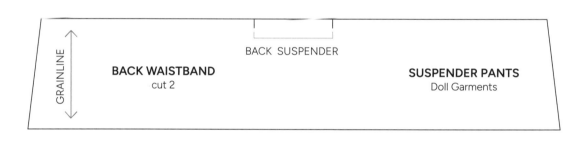

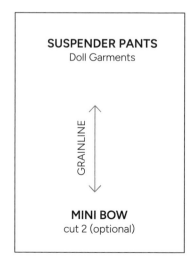

SEAM ALLOWANCE
⅜ in (0.9 cm) seam allowance included
unless otherwise specified

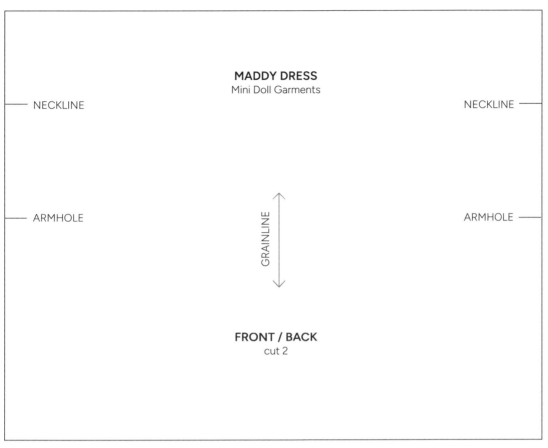

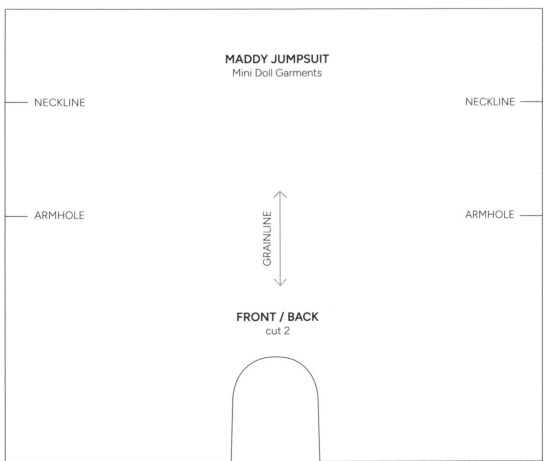

SEAM ALLOWANCE
⅜ in (0.9 cm) seam allowance included
unless otherwise specified

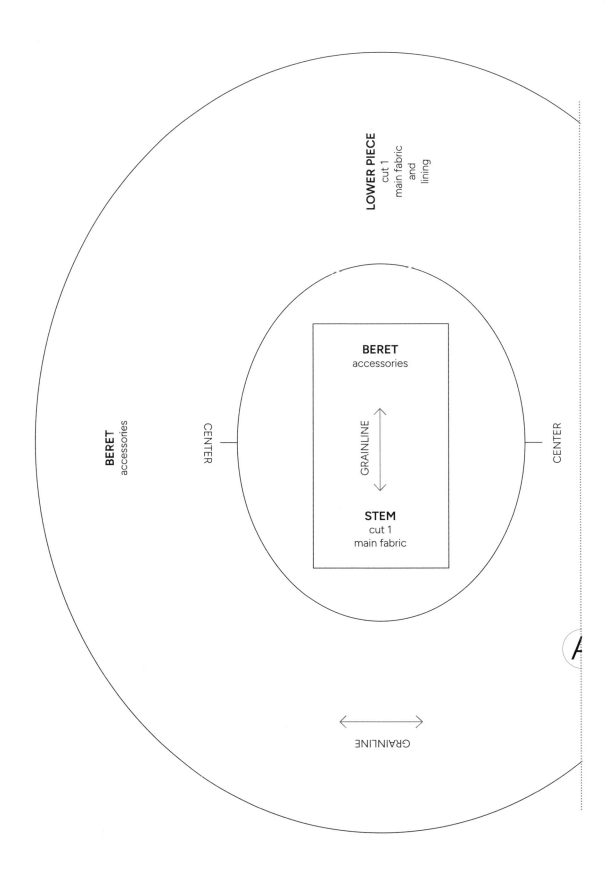

SEAM ALLOWANCE
⅜ in (0.9 cm) seam allowance included
unless otherwise specified

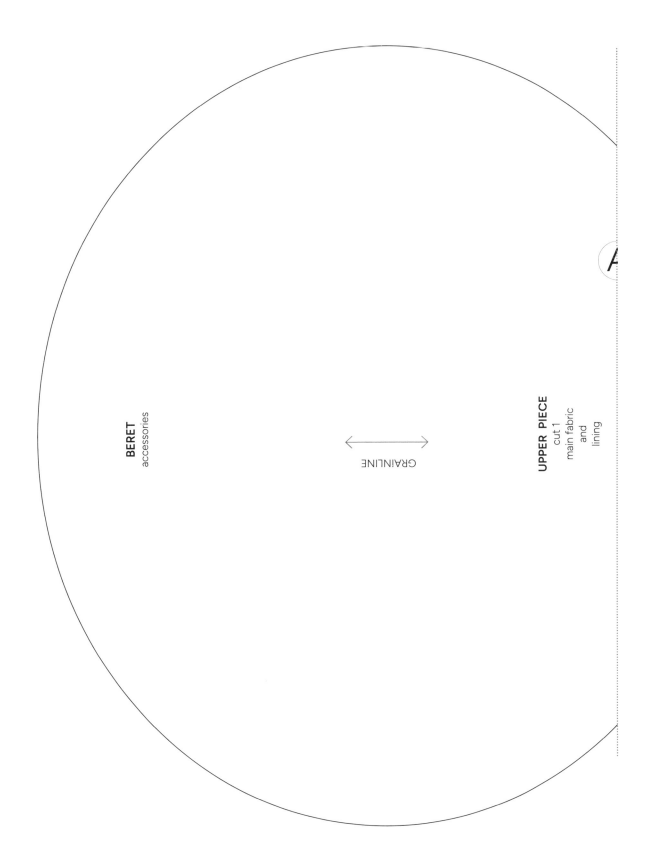

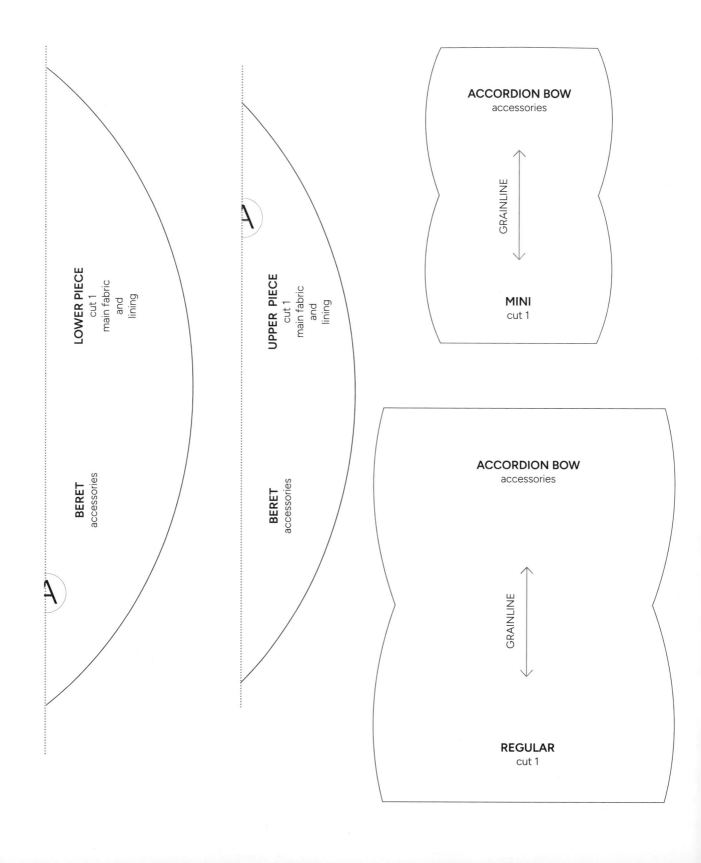